Robert J. Goldstein, Ph.D.

Angelfish

Everything About History, Care, Nutrition, Handling, and Behavior

Filled with Full-color Photographs and Illustrations

BARRON'S

CONTENTS

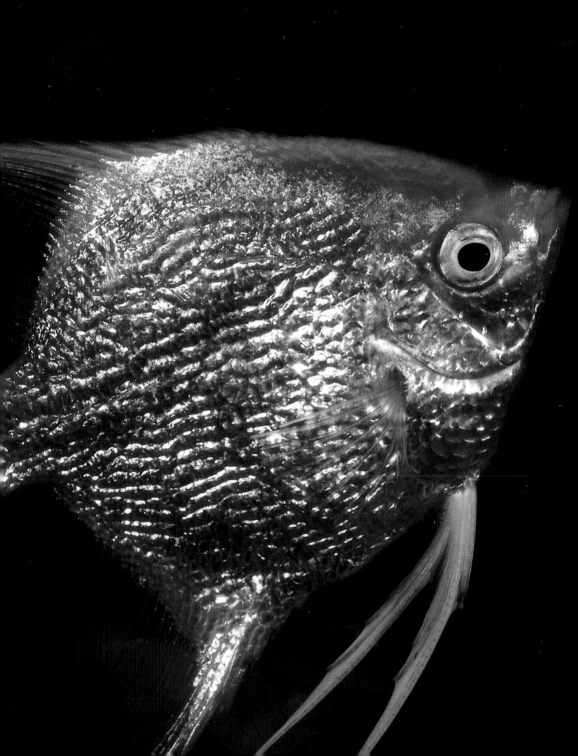

THE IDEAL FISH

Angelfish are among the first fish purchased for that first aquarium. As dime-sized bodies, they are inexpensive, active charmers that attack neither livebearer nor neon, gourami nor catfish. They are ideal community tank fish, are available in several color and finnage forms, and (compared to many other tropical fishes) are hardy enough for beginners.

Pterophyllum Scalare

The past 50 years of commercial and hobby breeding of *Pterophyllum scalare* have produced a hardy fish tolerant of common tap water conditions, a great range of temperatures, and resistant to diseases. We will never outgrow angelfish. Prominent and stately as adults, they are easy to breed and outstanding parents. Your entire surplus production of young will be snapped up eagerly by local pet stores to fill an insatiable demand from the public.

Pterophyllum scalare in the past has been known by other names (*P. eimekei*), and even today several populations of this fish are suspected to represent species not yet named by scientists. Two or more other species of angelfish (e.g., *Pterophyllum leopoldi, Pterophyllum altum*) are rarely imported. Among the reasons are restricted ranges, narrow seasons when they can be collected, and the high mortality of shipping wild fishes from soft, acid water (they tend to develop stress-related diseases). Economically,

Pearlscale angelfish, a recently discovered mutation.

these other angelfishes are not commercially competitive with the huge domestic supply of tank-bred *Pterophyllum scalare* in all its myriad varieties of finnage and coloration.

Although we have a good understanding of our domestic varieties of *Pterophyllum scalare*, confusion reigns over the identities of the valid *Pterophyllum altum* and *Pterophyllum leopoldi*, and over other fishes that go under the trade names of "red spot scalare," "Peruvian altum," "long-nosed angel," and "*Pterophyllum dumerilii*." What are those other fishes?

Cichlids

Cichlids aren't popular only with aquarists. They're a favorite of ichthyologists (fish scientists) who study their distribution, relationships, and even their behavior (ethology). Cichlids are modern fishes in evolutionary history, members of the Perciformes (perch-like advanced fishes), and among the most varied of all fishes. Cichlids occur throughout Central and South America and Africa, extend onto Madagascar, and reach even to the subcontinent of India.

The freshwater cichlids (family Cichlidae) resemble the marine damselfishes (family Poma-centridae). Cichlids have one pair of nostrils (there are two in damselfishes), unbranched hard spines, and branched soft rays in the dorsal, anal, and pelvic fins (you'd be surprised how many kinds of fishes have rays only), a particular number of rays in the tail fin (only an ichthyologist could care!), and a prominent lateral line often split into front and rear segments.

Early cichlids appear in the fossil record, so we know what they were like before the modern continents appeared, and we know how they spread and what extinct forms looked like. All this is engraved in ancient sedimentary rocks from different parts of the world. We know from the science of plate tectonics that these land masses were once joined. We also know how long ago cichlids first appeared, which ones persisted, gave rise to other types, or simply died out. All this information is as solid as the rocks in which their skeletons are etched forever.

The Geological Record

Our modern continents have not always been at their present locations. Early on, there was only a single supercontinent called Gondwana. It eventually broke up into Antarctica, Africa, North America, South America, Eurasia, and the Indian subcontinent. These modern continents were, and continue to be, carried in different directions by tectonic plates, portions of the planet's crust that float over the molten interior.

Other tectonic plates do not carry continents and remain hidden by the oceans. Contiguous tectonic plates spread apart, smash into one another, or ride under or over their neighboring plates, causing earthquakes and volcanic eruptions.

What happened and when is the science of geology. And since we also know when early fish happened, we can tell the history of fishes from the evidence in the rocks.

The Biological Record

So we can trace the origin of historic cichlids. But what of modern cichlids? How do we know when and how fast they evolved, and which ones are most closely or most distantly related? The modern tools of DNA analysis and computerized estimates of relationships have changed the field of classification (taxonomy).

Today we know how often genes mutate and which genes are shared by closely, distantly, or unrelated fish. Then we apply statistical programs to generate a most likely phylogenetic tree (tree of relationships of ancestors to their descendants and descendants to each other). We do this with DNA from chromosomes (inherited from both parents) and DNA from mitochondria (inherited only from the mother).

Chromosomal and mitochondrial DNA analyses, and computer-assisted phylogeny, all lead to the same conclusions. On top of that, we have better microscopes to study bone structures of modern fishes that can be compared with X-ray analyses of fossil fishes.

Total Evidence Analysis

Today there is a computerized statistical technique called total evidence analysis. It allows us to combine separate nuclear and mitochondrial DNA studies with studies of skeletons of fishes (osteology) and other kinds of investigations to produce a phylogenetic tree that once again resembles the results generated by any one of the techniques. With total evidence analysis, the statistical evidence is stronger because it's based on more information (more robust, as the scientists say).

What do geology, the fossil record, DNA analyses, osteological analyses, and total evidence analysis tell us about the history and relationships of cichlids? How do we know it's accurate? We keep testing alternative ideas and getting the same answers over and over. And why are we so smart? Maybe it's just that in the entire history of mankind, 95 percent of all the scientists who have ever lived are alive and conducting research today.

The First Cichlids

Cichlids first appeared 130 million years ago on Gondwana. Over time, Gondwana split into two, three, four, and more continents, a process that continues today. These fossil cichlids had spines in the fins, a single nostril, and other characteristics passed down to modern cichlids.

The early cichlids gave rise to the cichlids that survive today on the Indian subcontinent. Does that mean Asia also has cichlids? No. Long ago India and Madagascar were a single land mass. This mass split apart. The smaller piece drifted westward on a tectonic plate until it stalled off the east coast of Africa (the current island of Madagascar). The larger remainder was carried on another tectonic plate northward until it crashed into Asia and then kept on going. Today's India, Pakistan, and surrounding states of the Indian subcontinent are still pushing into Asia, forcing the growth of ever higher mountains where they collide (the Himalayas). That's why the cichlids of Madagascar are more closely related to *Etroplus* (the chromides) of India than

to the cichlids of Africa, and not far advanced over their early ancestors on Gondwana.

Primitive Cichlids

Madagascar is isolated. With almost no competitors, the early cichlids could exploit different habitats and foods, and today 18 species of their descendants occupy the island. On the Indian subcontinent, competition from southward spreading Asian fishes limited the early cichlids to narrow coastal zones, where today only three species of *Etroplus*-type descendants survive. The Indian and Madagascar cichlids of today are similar to the early stem cichlid of Gondwana.

Cichlids in Africa

We know the first cichlids appeared some 130 million years ago. Halfway through the history of cichlids, about 65 million years ago, as Gondwana was breaking up, a more advanced cichlid appeared resembling *Heterochromis* and *Hemichromis* of Africa.

While this *Heterochromis*-like fish was spreading over this large land mass, a giant crack was developing in the tectonic plate below, splitting it in two. As magma rose up, it pushed the plates apart and the land mass began breaking up, one side drifting eastward and the other westward. Between them, the Antarctic Ocean poured into the breach and the South Atlantic Ocean was born, separating the newly born continents of Africa and America. The primitive *Heterochromis*-like cichlid was now broken into two populations that would forever be separated.

As those land masses grew farther apart, other changes occurred. The ocean enlarged, and that early cichlid gave rise to new types.

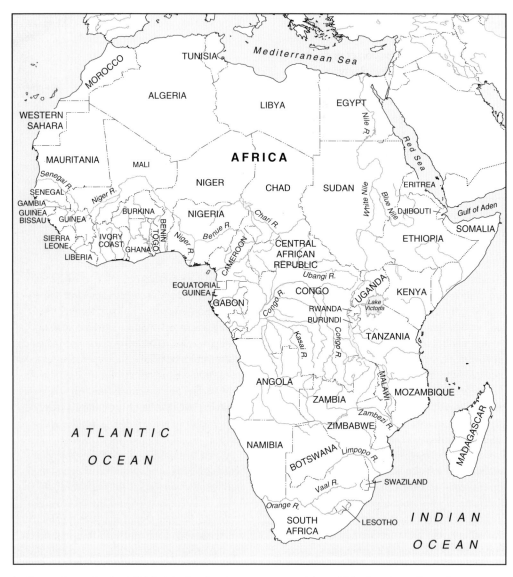

In the west, constant rainfall led to the development of great rivers. Here, Africa would see the modern *Hemichromis* (jewelfish) and similar cichlids (*Pelvicachromis*), *Lamprologus*, and so on evolving within the rivers. Parenting gave cichlids great advantages over other fishes that abandoned their eggs or fry, and cichlids spread into many habitats.

Discus fish are closely related to angelfish.

In northeastern Africa, something even more dramatic began to happen. Rainy years were intermittent, alternating with years of drought. Lakes became refuges for fishes to survive periods of decreased rainfall. Here, mouthbrooders, similar to *Tilapia*, evolved in response to fluctuating water levels. Again these cichlids had the advantage of being parenting fishes, able to move their eggs and young to safe locations as water levels fluctuated. Soon they were doing this irrespective of water levels. It was to be a fortuitous adaptation, for the worst was yet to come.

Soon the weakened plate below began to break apart and east Africa began breaking into subplates. As the split increased, Africa continued long-term climatic changes of drought alternating with excessive rainfall and flooding. As the land above the plates ripped apart, rain and rivers poured into the gouges in the Earth's crust to form the deep lakes known today as the Great Rift Valley lakes (Lakes Albert, Edward, Kivu, Malawi, and Tanganyika). A broad, flat area between two lines of the rift also became massive, shallow Lake Victoria.

During each period of drought, the giant lakes fragmented into isolated smaller lakes. Within each of these smaller lakes, the isolated *Tilapia*- and *Haplochromis*-like cichlid populations continued to change, adapting to the major foods, their teeth becoming modified for scraping algae (if that was the major food), plucking insects off the bottom or the top, attacking other fishes, or even mimicking other fishes for either protection or predation. The fluctuating water levels reinforced mouthbrooding as the most successful adaptation.

When the rains came again, the smaller lakes were flooded and reconnected. And the newer fish were different from the ones that had been isolated before. Over thousands of years of drought, flood, and the continued rifting of east Africa, the lake cichlids evolved at a spectacular pace compared to the cichlids of the central African rivers.

Additional Information

For a comprehensive view of the American cichlids and their distributions and habitats, see Staeck and Linke's two-volume series on American cichlids, available at your local pet shop.

For up-to-date technical information and new publications, Sven Kullander's web site at the Swedish National Museum *http://www.nrm.se/ve/pisces/acara/pterophy. shtml* is an essential starting point for understanding the evolutionary path that led to modern cichlids from their distant ancestors.

South American Genera of the Family Cichlidae (after Kullander)

Subfamily Retroculinae	*Retroculus*

Subfamily Cichlinae
Tribe Cichlini — *Cichla*
Tribe Crenicichla — *Crenicichla, Teleocichla*

Subfamily Astronotinae
Tribe Astronotini — *Astronotus*
Tribe Chaetobranchini — *Chaetobranchus, Chaetobranchopsis*

Subfamily Geophaginae
Tribe Crenicaratini — *Biotoecus, Crenicara, Dicrossus, Mazarunia*
Tribe Acarichthyini — *Acarichthys, Guianacara*
Tribe Geophagini — *Apistogramma, Apistogrammoides, Biotodoma, Geophagus, Gymnogeophagus, Mikrogeophagus, Satanoperca, Taeniacara,* "brasiliensis" group, "steindachneri" group

Subfamily Cichlasomatinae
Tribe Acaronini — *Acaronia*
Tribe Cichlasomatini — *Aequidens, Bujurquina, Cichlasoma, Cleithracara, Laetacara, Krobia, Nannacara, Tahuantinsuyoa,* "hoehni" group, "pulcher" group
Tribe Heroini — *Caquetaia, Heroina, Heros, Hoplarchus, Hypselecara, Mesonauta, Symphysodon, Uaru, Pterophyllum*

Cichlids in South and Central America

While the land mass carried eastward on its tectonic plate across the widening South Atlantic Ocean would become modern Africa, the other segment being carried westward would become modern South America.

Here, the *Heterochromis*-like ancestral cichlid would exploit the new continent through a *Retroculus*-like descendant. That basal *Retroculus* type persists today, but would give rise to successive lines leading to *Cichla, Astronotus* (oscar), *Geophagus* (eartheaters), *Crenicichla* (pike cichlids), and finally another and most recent line that led to *Cichlasoma* types and *Heros* types. All those lines persisted with modern representatives. The early *Heros* persisted to modern *Heros*, and also gave rise to *Symphysodon* (discus), *Mesonauta* (festivum), *Uaru*, and *Pterophyllum* (angelfishes).

Modern Cichlids

Modern cichlids today number about 1,000 species, half in Africa and half in Central and South America. Of perhaps 400 South American species of cichlids, approximately five (three named) are angelfishes.

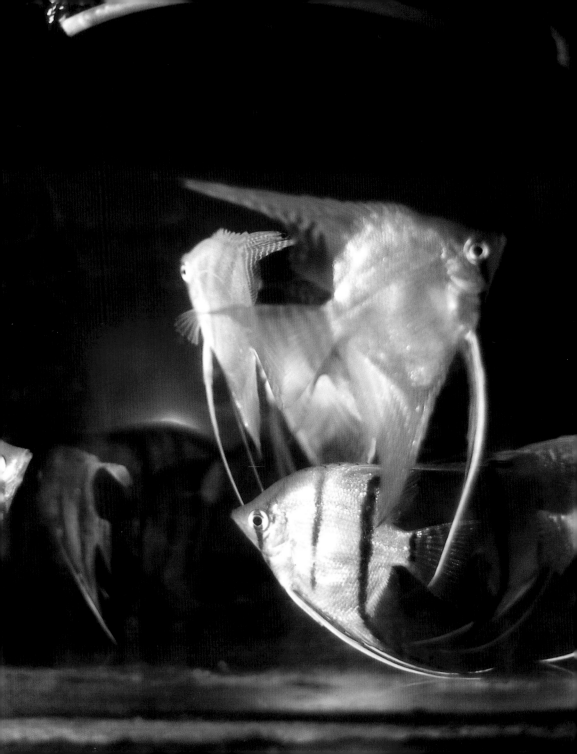

WILD ANGELFISH

In the scientific world, every fish is given a technical name. The first angelfish was described in 1823. Wild angelfish are distinguished by their physical traits and their habits.

How Fish Are Named

Every animal, including every fish, is given a two-part technical name, followed by the name of the person who proposed it, and the year in which the proposal was published. The first word of the technical name is the genus, the immediate group to which the fish belongs. The second word is called the specific (species) epithet.

A technical description of the fish must be published in a widely distributed journal (some aquarium magazines may qualify) and in enough detail that it may be readily distinguished from similar species. This technical description should include the place the fish was collected, its body proportions (morphometrics), and the numbers of spines and rays in its fins and scales along the lateral line (meristics). Tooth arrangement, gill structure, skeletal features, and even DNA analyses also might be included in the description.

One preserved specimen is donated to a major museum collection and labeled the "type" specimen, or holotype. The holotype is registered with an accession number so that future investigators can locate and examine it, should that

Wild angelfish at an importation facility in Miami, Florida.

be necessary. The legal name of the species is attached to that particular specimen.

If additional specimens are deposited, they get accession numbers as paratypes.

In the future another person might collect a fish resembling this one. Perhaps the newly found fish has a feature not mentioned in the description of the other fish, or it comes from a different river basin. Knowing the museum and accession number, the investigator can borrow that older preserved specimen and compare it with the fish he recently found. That way it's possible to decide if the two fish are the same or different, perhaps in ways not considered by the earlier scientist.

It's a fine system, but with limits. Sometimes type specimens are destroyed (during wars, for example), misplaced (it happens), or the locality information is vague. All three problems have occurred in the history of the names of angelfishes.

Names of Angelfish Species

The first angelfish to be described was named *Zeus scalaris* by the ichthyologist Lichtenstein in the year 1823. The name *Zeus*, however, had already been used for the genus name of another animal, and so a replacement genus name had to be coined.

That genus, *Pterophyllum*, was proposed by Heckel in 1840 to contain Lichtenstein's fish, and it remains in use today. Because the current genus name is different from the original genus name, the author and year of the original name are placed in parentheses, and the species is now written as *Pterophyllum scalare* (Lichtenstein, 1823).

Popular (non-scientific) literature (like this book) often leaves out the author and year, just reporting the fish as *Pterophyllum scalare*, but that's not allowed in technical literature. Another shortcut used in both popular and technical literature is using just the first letter of the genus name. And so, now that you know I'm discussing *Pterophyllum*, I can continue the discussion by calling the fish *P. scalare*.

After that first report by Lichtenstein, other investigators published reports of other new species. The names they proposed included *Plataxoides dumerilii* by Castelnau in 1855, and *Pterophyllum eimekei* by Ahl in a German aquarium magazine in 1928. (Obviously we can't use the abbreviation *P.* in the last sentence as it would be ambiguous.) *Pterophyllum altum* was described by Pellegrin in 1903 and *Pterophyllum leopoldi* by Gosse in 1963. In summary, we see that two old genus names (*Zeus* and *Plataxoides*) are no longer used, and the correct genus name for all species of angelfish is *Pterophyllum*.

By studying museum specimens, it has been determined that some of the specific epithets are no longer valid (*eimekei* and *dumerilii*) because these specimens were clearly identical to fish previously named (that makes the more

recent names junior invalid synonyms of the original or older name). Today the only valid epithets are *scalare*, *altum*, and *leopoldi*. Does this mean that there exist in nature just these three species of angelfish?

Modern Names

The status of the genus *Pterophyllum* was summarized in 2000 by Sven Kullander of the Swedish Museum of Natural History in Stockholm. According to Kullander, three species have valid names, but there may be more than three species. Of two additional names that had been in use, Kullander concluded that *Pterophyllum eimekei* and *P. dumerilii* were junior (invalid) synonyms of Lichtenstein's *P. scalare*, but that *P. altum* and *P. leopoldi* were valid and distinct species. There's more. Kullander noted that several undescribed and as yet unnamed species from different rivers have been confused with *P. scalare*.

Importers also have noted differences in angelfish populations that did not easily fit the descriptions of any of the three valid species. For example, there is a glittering or metallic angelfish in the hobby. Is this a new species? Is it *P. leopoldi*? And what is the so-called long-nosed angelfish? It is referred to by importers as *P. "dumerilii,"* but according to Kullander that name refers to *P. scalare*. It's also likely that some people are using the name *P. leopoldi* for more than one angelfish.

Kullander discussed the difficulty in determining the identity of the *P. scalare* originally described by Lichtenstein as the type specimens have been lost and we don't have the precise origin of the fish he described. We only know that the fish was collected from the Amazon River drainage of eastern Brazil. Kullander was sure that *P. eimekei* and *P. dumerilii* were this same fish based on their meristics and morphometrics, but his conclusions were based in part on earlier work of Dr. Leonard P. Schultz at the U.S. National Museum who might have accidentally mixed up several populations.

Angelfish populations called *P. scalare* occur in many places and differ in important ways. Various populations from lowland rivers of the Amazon drainage in Colombia and Brazil and from other rivers in Peru (central Ucayali River), French Guiana (Oyapock River), and Guyana (Essequibo River) may be distinct new species yet to be described and named.

How to Tell Them Apart

Many (not all) wild angelfish can be recognized by morphometrics, meristics, or pigment patterns. Although three species can be separated by meristics, the true number of species may be twice that many. For now, however, we can use Kullander's reported meristics to separate the three recognized species.

Ichthyologists usually count the number of scales in a horizontal line immediately above the lateral line, and the number of rows of scales from top to bottom above and below the lateral line. Angelfish species differ in the number of scales in the horizontal series.

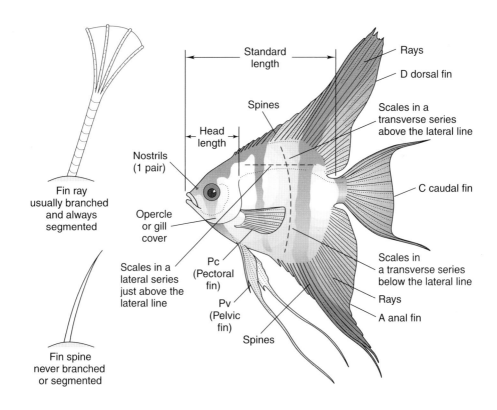

Fin ray usually branched and always segmented

Fin spine never branched or segmented

Standard length

Head length

Nostrils (1 pair)

Opercle or gill cover

Scales in a lateral series just above the lateral line

Pc (Pectoral fin)

Pv (Pelvic fin)

Spines

Spines

Rays

D dorsal fin

Scales in a transverse series above the lateral line

C caudal fin

Scales in a transverse series below the lateral line

Rays

A anal fin

Wild Pterophyllum scalare.

Wild type but domestically produced Pterophyllum scalare.

They also measure the number of hard, unbranched spines in each fin (using abbreviations such as "D" for dorsal fin, "A" for anal fin, "pc" for pectoral fin, "pv" for pelvic fin, and "C" for caudal fin). The spines are indicated with Roman numerals (XI). Behind the spines are the soft, branched rays, indicated with Arabic numerals (1,2,3). Angelfish species differ in the number of rays (not spines) in the dorsal and anal fins.

Because individual fish may vary, we measure the fin rays and scale counts of several fish from one locality (a single population) and compare the numbers with measurements from other localities. Despite some overlap, we see ranges of measurements useful for separating the species.

P. scalare is the **common angelfish** seen in pet stores. Wild fish range widely in the Amazon drainage from Brazil to Peru. These populations from Colombia, Guyana, and French Guiana may represent a mixture of species. Angelfish also have been reported from the Orinoco River drainage to north of the Amazon drainage.

Wild longnosed angelfish, possibly Pterophyllum leopoldi.

Natural barriers such as the Falls of the Iguaçu River near its confluence with the Parana River in Brazil prevent upriver dispersion of fishes.

Some angelfish imported from Georgetown, Guyana, which sits astride an area drained by neither the Orinoco nor the Amazon, also show some unique traits. One form is the **red-spot scalare** from the Rockstar area of the upper Demarara River in Guyana (many specimens have gold on top of the head). Guyana's rivers located between the Orinoco and the Amazon could hold new angelfish, which would not be surprising. A fish called the **Peruvian altum** is

Longnosed angelfish thought to be **Pterophyllum dumerilii**, *but is perhaps* **Pterophyllum leopoldi.**

not the true *P. altum*, but merely a morphometrically high-bodied *P. scalare* from the upper Amazon in Peru. Other fishes known as *P. scalare* probably will prove to be undescribed (new) species after their meristics, morphometrics, and distributions are carefully evaluated.

P. altum is a **giant angelfish** with a deeply indented snout profile almost at a right angle to the head, a high body, a doubling of the bands on the flanks (the intermediate bands not as distinct as the major bands), brown rather than black bands, and a high number of scales in a lateral series. It has been imported from small tributaries of the Rio Inirida, a tributary of the Orinoco in Colombia, from the Orinoco along the border of Venezuela with Colombia, and from the Rio Atabapo (upper Orinoco drainage).

TIP

Conditions for Wild Fish

Wild fish are easily frightened and should be disturbed as little as possible. They need to be housed in a high tank to accommodate their tall finnage, with soft and acidic water (reverse osmosis or deionized water filtered through peat moss). Security should be provided by abundant structure (rooted *Vallisneria* or *Sagittaria* plus waterlogged branches), dim, indirect light and a 24-hour night light, and privacy. Approach them slowly and infrequently, and place the aquarium out of a high traffic area. Adding rock salt to the water (1 tablespoon per 5 gallons [15 ml per 19 L]) assists breathing without increasing hardness.

The Three Recognized Species of Angelfishes

Name	Dorsal Rays	Anal Rays	Lateral Scales
P. scalare	23–29	24–28	30–40
P. altum	28–29	28–32	46–48
P. leopoldi	29–32	19–22	26–30

Kullander (personal communication) recalled *P. altum* from the upper Rio Negro, but probably not below the Sao Gabriel rapids, which is a barrier to the passage of many kinds of fishes. Further collections would be useful for validating and delimiting its distribution in the upper Rio Negro, and possibly even beyond the Sao Gabriel rapids toward the main stem of the Amazon. Apparently, it has not spread widely either in the Rio Negro or below, but it is widely distributed in the Orinoco drainage. (See also the chapter on *P. altum*.) Later on, we explain how stream capture of the Rio Casiquiare, originally a tributary of the upper Orinoco, has caused the Rio Casiquiare to reverse direction so that it is now a tributary of the upper Rio Negro. If this occurred recently (due to land subsidence), then *P. altum* could indeed now occur in both major rivers. If, on the other hand, stream capture is quite old, then it is likely that the Rio Negro and Rio Orinoco populations of *P. altum* are at least subspecies, and perhaps even separate species by now.

P. leopoldi was reported by one Miami importer to be shipped occasionally from Humaita on the Rio Madeira (Amazon River drainage) in central Brazil. Another importer, Marc Weiss, offered to eat all *P. leopoldi* from the Rio Madeira! Heiko Bleher reports that he

What Is a Species?

While a legal species is the name applied to the holotype specimen in a museum, a biological species is a potentially interbreeding population occupying a distinct region, and separated from other similar species by barriers that prevent interbreeding. That barrier could be a mountain, river, ocean, a breeding season, or simple lack of attraction. For fishes in close proximity, the barrier could be incompatibility of their genes so their hybrids do not survive, or the surviving hybrids cannot breed to produce fertile offspring.

For many years, species of fishes were described based only on meristics and morphometrics (for example, head length as a percentage of standard length, depth as a percentage of length, eye diameter as a percentage of head length). Patterns of pigmentation have only recently been used to identify and in some cases define species, although patterns fade or disappear in preservative. With advances in color photography and behavioral science, coloration became legitimatized as a defining characteristic.

Two decades ago, the mix of certain easily tested enzymes was incorporated into understanding whether populations were one or more species. These enzymes were variations on a single type, sometimes adapted to differing optimal temperatures. When the same functional enzyme occurs in different variations, the enzymes are called isozymes (iso=same). Isozyme analyses helped differentiate populations from different and isolated rivers as different species.

The most recent tool for differentiating species and subgroups is DNA analysis using a technique called polymerase chain reaction (PCR). PCR is based on taking a tiny amount of DNA from a fish and adding it onto the circular chromosome (or a chromosome part) of rapidly growing bacteria. As the bacteria rapidly reproduce, they create huge amounts of that DNA segment. With large amounts of identical DNA, the composition of the genetic makeup of two populations can be compared by ordinary laboratory techniques and, if sufficiently different, verified as coming from different species.

only found *P. leopoldi* in tributaries of the lower Rio Negro, where it joins the main stem of the middle Solimoes (the name of the central part of the Amazon River), and in the upper parts of the nearby Rio Purus, another tributary of the Rio Solimoes.

The name *P. leopoldi*, as used by hobbyists or people in the aquarium business, is not based on meristics (the only reliable measure), but on the presence of a dark interbar mark high on the flank. In my view, this marking is unreliable for identification.

P. leopoldi was also reported from the upper Essequibo drainage in Guyana to the east, but distance alone suggests it is a different fish. A glittering or metallic angelfish, sometimes imported, was thought to be the older adult of *P. leopoldi*, but that has not been confirmed either. It too may be an undescribed species. A form photographed by Hans Mayland (1995) appears to have undulating flank rows of blue and red reflective spots resembling the coloration of some wild discus fish (*Symphysodon discus*). As he did not count fin rays and scales,

Black zebra raised under continuous light.

Black lace raised under continuous light.

Wild caught P. scalare.

Cobra angelfish.

Wild angelfish vary in stripe density.

Wild P. altum.

Wild P. scalare.

Distribution of Angelfishes

Angelfishes occur in the Orinoco and Amazon rivers, and in smaller streams between these two huge basins. All angelfish streams drain into the South Atlantic Ocean.

The Amazon is the world's largest river and carries more water than any river on Earth. It disgorges eight times as much water as the Congo in Africa and twelve times as much as the Mississippi. Its tributaries include the Rio Negro, Rio Branco, Rio Madeira, and a hundred other major streams coursing through Peru, Ecuador, Colombia, Venezuela, Guyana, Argentina, Uruguay, and Brazil. No other river courses through so many countries. The headwater source of the Amazon is high in the frigid glacier region of the Andes, where five rivers converge on Nevado Mismi Mountain in southern Peru to become the most distant point from the mouth of the mighty Amazon.

the Rio Negro (Amazon River basin) along the Venezuela-Colombia border and shipped out of Manaus on the main stem of the Amazon. We don't know the identity of this fish, and after it is studied it may get a new name.

Waters

The rivers and backwaters of South America vary just as much as those in the United States. River water that flows through limestone highlands tends to be moderately hard, moderately basic (alkaline), cool, and clear. No angelfishes occupy these habitats.

Blackwater is the typical habitat of angelfishes. Largely slow-flowing, wide, meandering rivers of broad, flat forested river basins, these waters thunder from the sky during endless rainy seasons and leach through the surrounding forest and out of the ground the remainder of the year. The slow-moving water percolates through several feet of accumulated layers of leaves, twigs, branches, peat moss, and other vegetative debris and detritus, leaching tannic and humic acids, staining the water brown and yellow. Cations from underlying rocks are rapidly captured by the peats acting as ion-exchangers, and the water softens, with neither minerals nor alkaline reserve.

These clear, blackwater habitats are tea-colored, with pH often in the range of 4.3 to 6.0 (and even lower), no measurable hardness, barely measurable (if any) conductivity (perhaps 10–20 microSiemens), and no alkaline reserve (alkalinity). Zinc and mercury may occur at surprisingly high concentrations, the low pH perhaps leaching these heavy metals from the ancient peats, or perhaps these metals arrive here from great distances by atmospheric transport and deposition.

we cannot have confidence in his conclusion that it was *P. leopoldi.*

Frank Schäfer of the AquaLog series (personal communication) thinks *P. leopoldi* is the long-nose angel and the photo labeled *P. leopoldi* in AquaLog South American Cichlids 4 is an undescribed species. However, Kullander (personal communication) states that *P. leopoldi* can be recognized by its straight snout to dorsal outline and robust head, in addition to its scale counts.

P. "dumerilii" is considered a synonym of *P. scalare* by Kullander. However, importers are using the name for a fish they call the **longnosed angel** that is occasionally imported from

Another common habitat type is called white water habitat. White water refers to rivers traversing slopes so their waters erode the land and carry large silt loads. This turns the waters opaque. The clays making up the silt carry minerals derived from the underlying soil-forming rocks.

White waters (silt-laden waters) are usually neutral (pH 7.0) with moderate levels of dissolved calcium and magnesium cations making them slightly or moderately hard and conductive. These cations may be balanced by anions (carbonate, bicarbonate) creating an alkaline reserve (alkalinity) that buffers the water from acidification. Because these waters do not flow through peat forests, they retain their cations and do not pick up tannins and other stains. Angelfish are reported from white water only occasionally (as in Peru), but that is not a common angelfish habitat.

Structure

Their vertical markings tell you that angelfish live among bottom structure. They occur in quiet blackwater river backwaters or lakes amid tall rooted vegetation and submerged tree branches. Their narrow bodies and stripes provide camouflage and the ability to slip easily through brush piles. The vertically oriented vegetation provides protection, and serves as a substratum as they graze for food (aquatic insect larvae) and use for spawning.

Conditions

Are these conditions required? They are helpful for imported wild fish, but not required for domestic fish. Domestic fish do not need soft water. They spawn freely in hard, neutral, or alkaline water, in bare tanks and in high traffic areas if they have been raised under these conditions.

What are the best conditions for wild fish? Many fish found under restrictive conditions in nature do just fine when presented with entirely different conditions in captivity. *The habitat conditions in nature may not indicate the fish's requirements, but rather its tolerance of conditions not tolerated by its competitors and predators.* That said, wild angelfishes do not adapt well to conditions for domestic fish, and should be given dark, acidic, soft water conditions and dim light.

CARE OF ANGELFISH

Black angels and veiltails are more beautiful than plain banded or wild-type angelfish, but they are also more delicate. For your first angels, get plain wild-types with short fins and black bands on silver bodies. These, and the hybrid marble angels, are the most vigorous breeds.

Aquarium

A tropical fish beginner often starts with a 10-gallon (38-L) aquarium, but angelfish do better in tanks of at least 20 gallons (76 L). Height helps them avoid dragging their long anal and filamentous pelvic fins on the gravel, which leads to erosion of the skin, cuts, and infection. Show tanks (much higher than wide) provide the greatest height per unit volume, but that extra height requires more intense lighting to reach down to the rooted plants. The community tank may be equipped with an undergravel filter and 1½ to 2 inches (2 pounds per gallon) [4 to 5 cm (1 kg per 4 L)] of medium grade aquarium gravel. The gravel provides root space medium for plants, but has no other value and is a refuge for the accumulation of fecal wastes and dead plant debris. Tanks with rocks, gravel, plants, and other structures are difficult to keep clean.

Commercial breeders prefer bare tanks. Any plants are placed inside gravel-filled flower-pots easily moved for cleaning around them. Bare tanks are efficiently and quickly cleaned by siphoning out old water and the decomposing uneaten food on the bottom.

Light

A full hood provides light for plant growth and enjoyment of your fishes, retards water loss by evaporation, and keeps dust out and startled fishes inside the tank. The most popular lamps are full spectrum fluorescents with color enhancing wavelengths, but cheaper daylight bulbs are adequate for most tanks. A rule of thumb: the level of illumination for live plants is 10 watts per gallon, but lights are not required on a dedicated breeding tank. Lights set on automatic timers should come on after dawn (when the room is already illuminated) and turn off when you go to bed. A low wattage night light in the room helps prevent the fish from being startled at night (even walking around sends vibrations to the tank). Panic-driven fish may smash into the glass or leap from the aquarium and dry out on the floor.

Black angelfish raised under continuous (24-hour) light.

Temperature

Temperature control is unnecessary in warm climates, but helpful during winter in northern states. In addition to an aquarium heater (see page 35), the tank should contain an internal glass thermometer. Avoid stick-on digital thermometers that wear out and measure the air temperature more than that of the water; they are unreliable.

Filters

Filters provide mechanical removal of debris, chemical removal of dissolved gases and colored and toxic compounds, and (most important) water movement that enhances oxygen diffusion into the tank and carbon dioxide expulsion. Filters do not remove the end products of nitrogen (protein and nucleic acid) and metabolism (ammonia, nitrites, nitrates); that requires water changes.

For community tanks, the best filters are undergravel and some type of outside power filter, either a hang-on box type or a canister

TIP

Parts Per Million (ppm)

A part per million (ppm) is a cubic centimeter (cc), milliliter (ml), or milligram (mg) in a liter (L). A 4 ppm solution would be written as 4 ppm, 4 mg/L, 4 cc/L, or 4 ml/L. A liter is roughly the same as a quart, so 4 mg/L would be 16 mg per gallon (16 mg/gal). And a 1 ppm solution would be 4 mg or cc per gallon. Just think of ppm as mg or cc per quart and multiply by 4 to get gallons.

The Nitrogen Cycle

The principal waste products of fish metabolism are carbon dioxide and ammonia. Carbon dioxide is vented to the atmosphere if the water is well circulated. Ammonia is not, and can be lethal to fish even at concentrations as low as 0.02 parts per million (ppm).

After an aquarium has been set up for a month or more, the surfaces of the glass, gravel, filters, and other structures become coated with a microbial community called biofilm. The biofilm contains protozoans, bacteria, fungi, rotifers, minute crustaceans, nematode worms, and animals of which you've never heard. Among the bacteria are the nitrogen-metabolizers. One group takes up ammonia (NH_3) from the water and combines it with oxygen to make nitrites (NO_2), less toxic than ammonia but still dangerous for fishes. When the nitrite concentration builds up, another group of bacteria uses it to attach still another oxygen atom and make it into nitrates (NO_3) that are nontoxic to fish. Nitrates are plant nutrients and can stimulate the growth of rooted plants or, more often, noxious algae.

During the 4 to 6 week break-in period of an aquarium, when these nitrogen cycle bacteria are multiplying into large populations, the tank should only have hardy (nitrite-tolerant) and expendable (inexpensive) fish such as guppies and barbs. More demanding fishes, such as angelfish, should be deferred until the break-in period has passed.

filter that can be filled with a variety of media (floss, activated carbon, and clinoptilolite to remove ammonia). For breeding, bare tanks and sponge filters are preferred. For large scale

TIP

Percent Solutions

A percent solution is milligrams (mg) of a solid or milliliters (ml) or cubic centimeters (cc) of a liquid in 100 ml or cc of liquid (usually water). So, a 10 percent aqueous (meaning water) methylene blue solution would be 10 mg of methylene blue powder in 100 ml of water.

You can cut (dilute) a percent solution to any weaker strength if you have a clear vessel graduated in ml or cc. To make 70 percent alcohol from 95 percent alcohol, pour the 95 percent alcohol into the graduated vessel until it reaches the 70 (or 700) mark, and then top it off with water to the 95 (or 950) mark. To cut 70 percent alcohol to 10 percent alcohol, add 70 percent alcohol to the 10 (or 100) mark, and then top it off with water to the 70 (or 700) mark. You can cut any solution this way if you have a graduated container.

TIP

Formalin and Formaldehyde

Formalin and formaldehyde are not the same. A bottle labeled 40 percent (or 37 percent) formaldehyde refers to 40 or 37 milligrams of formaldehyde gas in 100 milliliters (about a tenth of a quart) of water. That bottle is called 100 percent formalin because it contains formaldehyde gas in saturation. If we want 10 percent formalin, then we cut it by adding nine parts of water; if we wanted 5 percent formalin, we would cut it with 19 parts of water. In practice, these measurements are crude approximations. For example, I often collect intestines, hearts, and gills of wild fish (in a jar), then pour hot water on them to rapidly kill and dislodge the parasites. I then look at how much water is in the container and add about 10 percent more of straight formalin, thereafter marking the specimen as preserved in 10 percent formalin.

operations, tanks may be plumbed in series for filtration with a single trickling filter.

Additional water quality protection is available with ultraviolet light (UV) canisters in series with other canister filters (as in the Rainbow Lifegard product line), or as stand-alone units.

Ozonizing units are not recommended because the buildup of excessive ozone can burn the skin and eyes of fish. Ozonizers require careful control through electronic units, may be undersized for safety, or restricted to sumps, where they can still pose a hazard.

Zebra leopard smokey.

Blushing marble angelfish.

Below: Wild type angelfish.

Black velvet.

Right: Wild
angelfish.

Butterfly angelfish.

HOW-TO: MAINTAINING

pH

Domestic angelfish do not do well in the soft or acidic water favored by wild angelfish. The easiest way to maintain a desirable pH and other parameters of high-quality water is through frequent, partial water changes.

The pH of the water is technically the negative logarithm of the hydrogen ion concentration. In simpler terms, it is the relative concentration of acid molecules (denoted by the H^+ part of water) and basic molecules (denoted by the ^-OH part of water). Acids and bases occur on more than water molecules. In addition to fish metabolism, decaying food from microbial growth puts other wastes into the water, including acids from bacteria growing on decaying food (or fish).

Municipal tap water is usually neutral, with the amounts of acidic and basic ions (H^+ and ^-OH) about equal. When this occurs, the pH is about 7.0, or halfway through the potential range of 0 to 14. (The pH cannot extend beyond those points.) In many parts of the country, the water flows through limestone, or calcium-laden rocks, making the water basic and the pH elevated.

Seawater, with 3 percent salts, has a pH of 8.3, for example. The limestone under Dallas, Texas provides groundwater that is unusually hard and basic, with a pH exceeding 8.0 on occasion. That's not a bad thing for angelfish, which thrive in hard, basic water. However, they also do well in neutral water (pH 6.8–7.2).

Water Changes

Weekly 50 percent water changes will produce fast-growing, healthy fish. No bacterial population, filter, or chemical can remove all growth-inhibiting nitrates and other chemical wastes in an aquarium. Professional breeders often change 80 to 90 percent of the water every other day. Growth and health depend far more on water changes (that remove growth inhibitors and toxins) than on the frequency or quality of feedings. And water changes are the easiest way to maintain neutral pH.

Hard and Soft Water

Hard and soft denote the concentrations of cations in water. These cations (positively

Siphoning water from the aquarium is the most efficient way to perform a water change. If the aquarium is quite large, siphoning the water out, via a garden hose, into the yard or sink is recommended. For a small aquarium, siphon the water into a bucket first, then dispense of the water elsewhere. Always siphon from the bottom of the aquarium, particularly if you have an undergravel filter and are using a gravel vacuum.

charged ions) are mostly calcium (Ca⁺) and magnesium (Mg^+) with lesser amounts of other cations, and they are often associated with anions (negatively charged ions) such as hydroxides (^-OH) and sulfates ($^-SO4$). The higher the concentration of dissolved cations in water, the greater the hardness. Rainwater, distilled water, and deionized water all have almost no cations and are considered soft.

What is the importance to aquarists? Hard water also contains calcium ions that assist the transfer of oxygen and carbon dioxide across the gill membranes, making it easier on fish respiration so they do less work. Sodium ions (Na^+) work the same way. That is why aquarists often add a tablespoon of salt (NaCl) to each 10 gallons of water. When bacteria decompose leftover food (or dead fish), they release acids from metabolism, and if there are no anions or bases (^-OH, $^-SO4$) to combine with and neutralize these acids, a problem in soft water, the bacterial acids acidify the entire aquarium. With its hydroxides and sulfates, hard water more easily buffers against the bacterial acids and resulting drop in pH. It's a no-brainer that hard water is better than soft water for domestic angelfish.

How hard? I've never run into water too hard for domestic angelfish. If you're concerned, use a hardness test kit or call your municipal water plant for an analysis of the local tap water. You can dilute hard tap water with bottled distilled or deionized water from your supermarket, but in my view, the harder the water the better, unless it contains other noxious chemicals.

Measuring Tools

You can measure temperature, pH, chlorine, ammonia, nitrite, nitrate, and other water

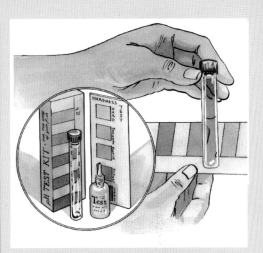

Regular maintenance should include testing for ammonia, nitrate, nitrite, pH, and hardness.

quality parameters with glass or electronic instruments, liquid test kits, or test paper strips. Today's paper strips have high reliability and longer shelf lives than liquid test kits. Any kit more than a year old is probably unreliable and should be replaced. Thermometers and heaters are reliable the first year, but risky thereafter. Paper test strips should be stored dry in the refrigerator to extend shelf life. Electronic meters have high accuracy, but should be regularly calibrated with standard solutions or with their internal standards.

For measuring chemicals, use a tall measuring cup from a grocery store or a one liter (L) (about the same as a quart) graduated cylinder from a scientific supply house. The graduated markings indicate tenths, hundredths, and thousandths of a liter. A thousandth of a liter is a milliliter (ml), which is the same as a cubic centimeter (cc).

PURCHASING ANGELFISH

Most people buy small, inexpensive dime- or nickel-sized fish and raise them to adulthood. Young fish adapt more easily than older fish to new environments, new foods, new lighting, and even a wider temperature range than adult fish.

Angelfish are inexpensive and cute when their bodies are nickel- or dime-sized, but they don't remain small. Because they grow rapidly, the absolutely smallest tank for adults is 15 gallons (57 L). Of course, they do better in 20- and 30-gallon (76- and 133-L) tanks, and if you are serious about raising them and even breeding them, start with an appropriately larger aquarium. If your only home aquarium is a 5- or 10-gallon (19- or 38-L) tank, delay purchasing angels, and select other fishes like tetras, danios, dwarf cichlids, or livebearers that don't require much room.

If your goal is to see them breed and raise a family, you'll need to have at least one male and one female.

Making the Selection

How many fish should you buy? Unlike livebearers, there are no external markings or structures to help you determine sex. So you have to get enough fish to increase the odds of getting a pair. If you buy two fish, the odds are 50 percent that you'll get a pair and 50 percent that you will not. Scientists have calculated that six fish provide a 95 percent probability of having at least one pair. Of course, those six could turn out to give you two or three pairs, and in fact getting two pairs occurs quite often.

How do you select fish from the pet store? Cost is one factor, but health and vigor are more important. After all, weak or unhealthy fish may fail to survive and grow, and are no bargain. Look for tanks that contain only angelfish, and only angelfish all of the same size. Angelfish mixed with other kinds of fishes like mollies or platies (often raised outdoors in ponds) might be infected from diseases carried by the other fishes, diseases that won't become obvious for a week or more. And angels of mixed sizes in one tank are grounds for suspecting that the tank has been restocked with several batches over time, a practice that also risks introducing a disease if the different batches came from different suppliers.

Bagging

The dealer will put your fish into a plastic bag and may add green or blue medication to

Clown angelfish.

relax the fish and kill common external parasites. Of course, not all medications work on all
diseases, so the treatment is a precaution, but
not a guarantee. Some dealers don't add medications because they have great confidence in
pretreatments and ongoing care the fish
received while in their care. These dealers often
guarantee the fish to live a day or a week and
replace any that die in that time.

The dealer may add compressed oxygen to
the bag (or simply air if he doesn't have oxygen) before sealing the bag. Don't be concerned if the sealed bag contains 3 or 4 times
as much air or oxygen space as it does water.
The fish need very little water, only enough to
keep their skin and gills immersed. It's more
important to have a large void space above the
water into which carbon dioxide gas can
escape. The oxygen in the void space diffuses
back into the water as the fish use up the
water's oxygen.

Does it matter if the dealer has oxygen or
air? Probably not. Air contains 21 percent oxygen, and that's quite a high concentration compared to the oxygen in water, which rarely
exceeds eight parts per million parts of water
(8 ppm). Air is 21 parts per hundred (21/100,
21 pph, 21 percent). Do the math, and you'll
see that even air has far more oxygen than
water and will quickly diffuse into the water
(from the higher concentration into the lower
concentration). The same is true with carbon
dioxide. It will diffuse from water with the
higher concentration (from fish respiration)
into the air (which has almost none of its
own). Do fish die from lack of oxygen? Almost
never. What kills them is too much carbon
dioxide if it cannot escape to a void space
above the water.

Unbagging

You've picked out six plain angels and taken
them home. Don't simply dump them
into your tank. Angelfish are sensitive to bright
lights and temperature changes. Do as the
dealers do. Turn off the room (and tank) lights,
and float the plastic bag of angelfish in the
aquarium for a half hour. During this time
the temperature of the water in the plastic
bag will change to the temperature of the
water in your tank.

Now open the bag, spill off some bag water
into a bucket, and replace it with tank water.
It's important for disease prevention to intro-
duce the least amount of pet shop water with
the new fish. Let the bag float another five
minutes, and then again discard some water
from the bag and replace it with more tank
water. Repeat this discard and replace exercise
4 or 5 times. By this time any differences in
water quality (hardness, pH, other chemical
characteristics) have disappeared, and the fish
have been adapted gradually to your tank
water rather than exposed to a sudden change.

Should you now dump the remaining water
with the fish into the tank? It's a better idea to
net the fish from the bag so that no pet shop
water at all gets into your tank. Not everyone
is this careful but, like washing your hands
after going to the bathroom, it's good hygiene
that might prevent the transmission of a contagious disease.

The lights should be left off and the fish not
fed until the following day. That allows them to
learn their new environment in dim light
(which is less stressful) and gives their stomachs
a chance to settle down. That first night they
will go to sleep a bit hungry. The next day they
will wake up gently as dawn lights the room of

their new tank, and they will have a healthy appetite. The time to put the tank light on is when the fish are wide awake and will not be frightened by sudden bright illumination.

Temperature

Domestic angelfish do best in clean, clear water of moderate hardness and neutral to slightly basic pH (6.8–7.4). They are at their best at temperatures of 76 to 82°F (25 to 30°C).

Temperature may be controlled by a thermostatically controlled aquarium heater or a warm room. The most reliable aquarium heaters can fail. A heater slightly undersized for your aquarium is much safer. The industry recommendation is 5 watts of heat-generating capacity per gallon (4 L), so a 20-gallon (76-L) tank would require a 100-watt heater. I recommend undersizing to the next size down. If your tank should warrant a 100-watt heater (20-gallon [76-L] size), give it a 75-watt unit. This is enough to take the chill out of the water and, should the thermostat fail, the heater will be unable to cook your fish. An alternative solution is to use two 50-watt heaters; again, if one fails it will not be fatal to your fish.

Water Changes

Water quality is as important as temperature, but more difficult to control. Every time food is put in a tank, it is digested by the fish or by microbes to waste products that include ammonia and other nitrogenous compounds related to urine. What goes in, must come out. Those waste products accumulate in your tank water. They must be removed or they will weaken the fish, stunt their growth, tint the water yellow, and make the fish susceptible to disease.

Filters can remove particles of sediment and algae, and carbon in the filters can remove colors and some chemicals from the water, but no filter is perfect. To maintain high-quality water, you must regularly remove polluted water and replace it with new clean water. That clean water comes from your tap and has been treated by your local water purveyor (usually the municipality) to remove nitrogen compounds and all other noxious substances. Tap water is cleaner than almost any kind of natural water.

The tap water should be chemically dechlorinated and allowed to sit in a barrel or bucket while the temperature equilibrates to room temperature. At the same time, supersaturated air diffuses out of solution and accumulates as bubbles on the sides and bottom. Cold tap water contains more air than water at room temperature, so allowing it to rest and warm up will cause the water to release its excess air. Were you to put that water directly into your tank, the bubbles might attach to your fish and damage their eyes or gills by drying and oxidizing (burning) them.

Are filters useless? Not entirely. Their removal of drifting particles and color from the water, and their vigorous circulation of the water, all enhance water quality, so filters have a useful role in any aquarium. The danger is over-reliance on filters by taking the claims of manufacturers too seriously. A filter is only an adjunct to frequent, partial water changes (50 percent or more a week), and not a substitute.

Foods and Feeding

Angelfish are carnivores that eat insects, worms, and crustaceans, but not plants or

Blushing smokey angelfish.

fatty acids (HUFAs). For growth of juveniles (grow-out), breeders wean the young off expensive brine shrimp nauplii and onto enriched dry foods (flakes or granules). The home aquarist wants a single dry food (for convenience) suitable for most of his community tank fishes, and dry foods are convenient. Not all are nutritious, so foods should be selected based on ingredients. (Fry foods are discussed in the chapter on breeding angelfish.) Foods for juvenile and adult angelfish fall into the categories of dry, freeze-dried, and live foods.

Dry Foods: A commercially successful food must have three attributes. It must be attractive to the buyer, attractive to fish, and it must be good for fish. What is attractive to the fish or buyer has nothing to do with nutritional value. For example, foods packaged as suitable for herbivores are often colored green; those hawked as rich in brine shrimp or worms are red, and those claiming rich amounts of egg yolk will be yellow. The colors of these niche market foods result in part from the addition of food coloring agents. The colors simulate and suggest high concentrations of important ingredients. The package often has a profusion of colors. Many consumers pay a premium for foods with colorful packaging, or that carry an aura of expertise (German foods, Japanese foods). But all nations use the same nutrition science in their aquaculture, and the only package information that counts are the ingredients and their order. (Ingredients are listed in order of their percentage in the formula.)

seeds. They may also eat slow-swimming, small fishes. The small invertebrates are rich in fats and proteins (about 50:50) and almost devoid of carbohydrates and fiber. In the wild, angelfish feed casually and lightly all day long. What should we feed them in captivity, and how often should they be fed?

Live and frozen animal foods provide the richest and most natural diet for angelfish. Breeders offer them adult brine shrimp (live or frozen) and frozen bloodworms at least once a day, and usually more often. A diet rich in fats is important for egg development. Newly hatched angelfish fry are started on live baby brine shrimp (*Artemia* nauplii), sometimes enhanced with fish oils containing highly unsaturated

The same dry ingredients can be found as floating or sinking flakes, twigs, granules, pellets, or some other form. Angelfish readily feed from the surface, so floating foods are appropriate. Flakes are the least advisable dry food because they fragment readily, and the particles are decomposed by bacteria and fungi, resulting in degraded water quality. Flakes are usually the least expensive dry food and, for this reason, preferred by commercial breeders for grow-out and maintenance diets.

Commercial dry foods may be attractive to your fish because of appetite stimulants such as garlic extract and certain amino acids. When fish voraciously consume dry food, it only means the food tastes or smells good. (Children stuff themselves with candy, but that doesn't mean it's good for them, and I've never seen a child voraciously attack a plate of cauliflower.)

Ignore the packaging hyperbole and read the detailed list of ingredients. Dry foods for angelfish should have a meat as the first listed ingredient (rich in proteins and fats) rather than a grain (mostly carbohydrate). The first and second listed (and most abundant) ingredients should be fish meal and shrimp meal. A mix of meats assures a range of amino acids and fats, so look for other meat components such as worms, krill (zooplankton), insects, clam, squid, mussel, oyster, beef or chicken heart or liver, or simply seafood.

Certain substances are rich in HUFAs (e.g., fish liver oil, krill, shrimp), color enhancers (*Spirulina*, astaxanthin, paprika, peppers), or fat soluble vitamins (fish liver oil, egg yolk), B-vitamins (torula or other kinds of yeast), other essential substances (vitamin mixes), and ingredients that prolong shelf life. "Antioxidant" is an ambiguous term that can refer either to nutritional substances that eliminate free radicals in the body, or substances that prevent oils and fats from becoming rancid (oxidized).

In a Hawaii Sea Grant study comparing growth rates of angelfish on different diets, commercial trout chow outperformed a leading aquarium flake food. I've also found commercial trout chow granules to provide better growth than flake foods.

Freeze-dried foods: Freeze-dried zooplankton (krill) are rich in proteins and fats, including HUFAs, but they are dusty and should be sifted before feeding. The dust should be saved as food for newly hatched fry. Freeze-dried bloodworms induce allergic reactions in some people. Freeze-dried tubifex worms are associated with municipal sewage containing fecal bacteria.

Frozen foods: The most commonly used frozen foods are adult brine shrimp (crustaceans) and bloodworms (Chironomidae, a family of insect larvae). In large quantities (two pound lots) they cost about the same. Frozen brine shrimp are rich in proteins and taste-enhancing amino acids. Frozen bloodworms are rich in proteins, fats, and oils, are more nutritious than brine shrimp, but are not eaten as ravenously. A good diet for angelfish is a mix of both, at the same or alternate times. Frozen mysid shrimp is an exceptionally nutritious food, but also exceptionally expensive. It is useful for weaning imported wild fish onto frozen foods.

Other frozen foods include seafood meats and marine algae marketed to marine aquarists. Marine algae have no nutritional value for freshwater angelfish. (Saltwater angelfish are omnivores in a different fish family.) Many seafoods are rich in fats and proteins, and make excellent dietary supplements. You can purchase frozen seafoods at a pet store or make your own at a fraction of the cost. The premier seafood is edible shrimp. Whole fresh shrimp from your supermarket should be frozen with or without the shell, and the frozen blocks shaved for feeding directly to your fish. Other nutritious seafoods include oyster, clam, scallop, and squid. Frozen finfish (tuna, ocean perch, and so on) have less nutritional value for angelfish, and may contain tendons that can cause choking. Frozen fish roe is exceptionally nutritious, and helps condition fish for breeding.

Live foods: The following live foods are good for adult angelfish:

✔ Adult brine shrimp (*Artemia*) are collected from salt drying ponds on the West Coast and grown in greenhouses in Florida for the East Coast market. Brine shrimp thrive in saline waters. They are rich in proteins, but not particularly rich in fats. Angelfish consume them greedily. Live brine shrimp from the West Coast should be stored in open, shallow containers in the refrigerator; those from Florida should be kept at room temperature with aeration, but will die if chilled.

✔ Tubifex worms (*Tubifex* and its allies in the Tubificidae) are collected from municipal or industrial wastewater treatment plant effluent streams, where they occur in muddy shallows in wavy, red colonies. Most live tubifex today is collected from Mexico, and may be contaminated with human fecal bacteria. Tubifex should be stored under slowly running cold tap water for cleaning and survival.

✔ Blackworms are larger coldwater Tubificidae collected from the effluents of trout farms and the wastewater treatment lagoons of food canneries. Any tubificid might carry larval tapeworms that can infect suckers and minnows, but they do not infect angelfish.

✔ Earthworms (*Lumbricus*) are excellent live foods for adult angelfish. Earthworms can be dug from your own backyard, induced to come out of the dirt by spilling salty water on the ground, or collected from damp leaf or mulch piles. Large worms are chopped or cut into smaller pieces and small ones fed whole. Many earthworms can survive a day or more under water in aquariums with good aeration. Excess earthworms can be stored in damp leaves or peat moss. You can also purchase them at fishing tackle (bait) stores, or grow them in a bed of peat moss and soil with damp bread or cornmeal as food. Wild earthworms are sometimes purged by feeding them cornmeal prior to use as fish food.

✔ *Daphnia* species (water fleas) are sometimes available at pet stores, and can be grown outdoors in barrels and pools by feeding them green water or yeast slurry. They are not meaty or nutritious for large fish such as angelfish, but help provide water quality control in fry tanks through their constant feeding on algae, bacteria, and protozoans. *Daphnia* should be kept at room temperature until use.

✔ Glassworms (*Chaoborus*) are nutritious insect larvae that collect in northern ponds in winter. They should be stored in the refrigerator until use, and will survive in warm aquaria until eaten.

Live blackworms, tubifex worms, glassworms, brine shrimp, and *Daphnia* are sold at many pet stores. Live earthworms are sold at fishing bait and tackle shops. Starter cultures and directions for *Daphnia*, white worms, grindle worms, and fruit flies—all excellent live foods for angelfish—can be purchased through classified advertisements in aquarium magazines. Ads for starter cultures of red wiggler earthworms appear in fishing magazines.

Supplements: Many nutrients play important roles in the growth, sexual maturation, and breeding of large fish, and enhance survival and growth rates of larval fish. No group is more important than the lipids or fats. Natural and synthetic foods consist mainly of protein (meat), lipid (fats and oils), carbohydrate (sugars and starches), and ash (bone and other minerals). In the body these raw materials are released through digestion, and broken down into elementary units consisting of almost 20 kinds of amino acids, a smaller number of simple sugars like glucose, and many simple lipids such as fatty acids. Then these small components are built up into the materials needed by the fish for structures and functions (muscle, bone, hormones, digestive juices, and so on).

All these chemical changes are catalyzed by enzymes that also must be built from precursors. Many enzymes consist of two parts—a protein the fish can make and another substance that must be included in the diet. Many enzymes also require a cofactor, much of which the fish can make, but again including a portion it needs preformed and in the diet. In addition, many of the proteins and fats in a fish's body (especially the brain) cannot be made entirely from precursors. Two groups of the most important of these substances are the carotenoids and the long-chain unsaturated fatty acids.

Carotenoids: You know them as vitamin A, beta-carotene, astaxanthin, xanthophyll, and a few other names. They are a part of many enzymes and other proteins, and because they cannot be made from precursors, they must be included in the diet. They enhance red and orange colors, and the survival and growth rate of baby fish. You can enhance your own prepared

Dodecahexaenoic acid, a HUFA or highly unsaturated fatty acid

$H_3C - CH = CH = CH = CH_2 - CH = CH - CH = CH - CH = CH - COOH$

foods, and even increase the nutritive value of live baby brine shrimp, by adding a cheap source of carotenoids: ordinary kitchen paprika.

The highly unsaturated fatty acids, or HUFAs, are long-chain versions of fatty acids. Simple fatty acids might contain just 2 to 8 carbon atoms in a line, but the long-chain acids might have 18 to 24 carbons. Fatty acids can be saturated or unsaturated, and this refers to whether each carbon atom is singly or doubly bonded to its neighbor, as in C-C or C=C. If it has double bonds, it is called unsaturated. If it has a lot of carbons (a long-chain fatty acid) and a lot of double bonds, it is a HUFA. Certain HUFAs are important elements of brain and other nerve tissues and cannot be synthesized from precursors. They must be included in the diet. You can put HUFAs in foods by adding inexpensive cod liver oil.

Other important nutrients are the complex B-vitamins found in dried or living yeast. Microworm cultures are rich in live baker's yeast (and an excellent food for baby fish), but all yeasts are good B-complex supplements for prepared foods.

The addition of yeast, paprika, and cod liver oil in minute quantities to prepared foods, and even to live baby brine shrimp cultures an hour before they are to be harvested for food, will vastly increase the nutritive value of these foods and the survival and growth rates of your baby fish. They also will enhance the growth of older fish.

GENETICS

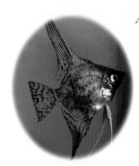

Angelfish traits are controlled by genes, segments of deoxyribonucleic acid (DNA). Every angelfish has hundreds of thousands of genes located in chromosomes in the nucleus of every cell. Angelfish have many chromosomes, and all exist in pairs.

Inheritance

The chromosomes occur in pairs, one of each pair contributed by the mother and one by the father. And so the genes on the paired chromosomes also represent contributions from the mother and the father. We don't know which genes occur on which specific chromosomes, but the locations are consistently in one part of one particular chromosome (and its equivalent paired chromosome).

Mitosis and Meiosis

All the cells of the body divide through mitosis. In mitosis, the pairs of chromosomes double (so there are four of each chromosome rather than two) before the cell divides, pulling apart to form two daughter cells. As the cell divides, the four chromosomes in each set are shared by the daughter cells, each getting, once more, the original paired condition of one chromosome from each parent. This paired condition of chromosomes is called diploid

Leopard angelfish carrying the smokey and zebra genes.

(double), and is the normal condition of cells. It is symbolized as $2n$.

The sex cell precursors also undergo mitosis. But when the animals become sexually active, some of them undergo another process to produce eggs and sperm, a process called meiosis. Meiosis results in each egg or sperm cell getting only one member of a chromosome pair from each parent. In meiosis, the chromosomes do not double (to produce sets of four) before being divided between the daughter cells (eggs or sperm). And so the egg or sperm cell has only half as many chromosomes as its parent cell. This condition is called haploid, and is symbolized as n. When the haploid (n) sperm nucleus fuses with the haploid (n) egg nucleus during fertilization, the resulting new individual (zygote, soon to become embryo) is diploid ($2n$), with all its genes now in pairs. From this point, until it too reaches sexual maturity, all its cells will undergo only mitosis.

Dominant or Recessive?

When two different genes occupy precisely the same position on chromosome pairs, they are called alleles. Wild *Pterophyllum scalare* look much alike. But alleles can arise through mutations, when the DNA making up a gene is reorganized and the gene produces a different outcome. An example of a mutation in angelfish is the gene resulting in long fins (instead of normal fins). When an angelfish inherits two allelic genes, one of the genes may mask the effect of the other gene, or dominate it. Such genes are called dominant genes. Or, it may blend with or only partially mask the other gene, and in that case it is called an incompletely dominant (blending) gene. Long fins is such a gene in angelfish, and it is symbolized as V (for veiltail) with a capital letter because it is, at first blush, dominant to wild-type, symbolized as +. If it were masked by (recessive to) wild-type, we would use a small letter instead of a capital. Capital and small letters are used to indicate dominance or recessiveness of alleles to the wild-type and sometimes to each other.

We know that V is incompletely dominant because, while V+ gives us a longfinned fish, VV gives us an extra-longfinned fish. If veiltail were completely dominant (instead of incompletely dominant), you could not tell the difference between a VV and a V+ fish.

A longfinned angelfish can have either of two conditions for the gene for long finnage. Its gene pairs might be V+ or VV, the first indicating that only one parent carried the longfin gene and the second indicating that both parents carried that gene. In the case of V+, we say that the fish is heterozygous for the longfinned gene (hetero=different).

In the second case, VV, the parent is homozygous (homo=same). Let's look at what happens when both the male and female are homozygous for the gene. During meiosis, only one gene of each pair from each parent goes into each egg and each sperm cell because the pairs of chromosomes are divided from $2n$ into n.

Punnet Squares

We can anticipate the odds of each type of sperm cell gene combining with each type of egg cell gene during fertilization.

		V	(male)
(female)	V	VV	

We can illustrate the proportions and possibilities of the offspring from the parents by using a box called a Punnet Square. When any egg combines with any sperm, the only possible combinations will be

		V	V (male)
	V	VV	VV
(female)			
	V	VV	VV

Here, VV is the genotype (genetic makeup) of the offspring represented by the fertilized egg (zygote or first stage of an embryo). The (homozygous) extra-longfinned male crossed with an extra-longfinned female will yield all (homozygous) extra-longfinned offspring.

Suppose we want to cross an extra-longfinned male with a normal wild-type (shortfinned) female. V represents the dominant longfinned gene, and + represents wild-type.

	V (male)
(female) +	$V+$ (offspring)

In this case, the offspring still appear as ordinary longfins. They are genotypically a combination of V and +, and their fins are longer than the wild-type, but shorter than the extra-longfinned angelfish. What they look like is called their phenotype, and what they consist of genetically is called their genotype.

Suppose you got a pair of angelfishes with long fins from somebody but were not sure if they were $V+$ or VV. If they were VV, all of their offspring would be extra-longfinned (VV). If both parents were $V+$, then you would get a mixture of approximately 25 percent extra-longfinned to 50 percent longfinned to 25 percent shortfinned fish. Here is how it works.

	V	+ (male)
V	VV	$V+$
(female) +	$V+$	++

In angelfish, because albinism is recessive to wild-type, it would be symbolized with a small a. A carrier of the albino gene would be $+a$ and appear normal, while only a fish carrying a pair of albino genes, aa, would in fact appear albinistic. If you crossed two carriers of the albino gene, you would get one albino to three normal-appearing fish, with two of the three normals being carriers of the albino gene.

	+	a (male)
+	++	$+a$
(female) a	$+a$	aa

If you crossed an albino with a carrier, then half the offspring would be albino and half would be carriers.

	a	a (male)
a	aa	aa
(female) +	$a+$	$a+$

Gold color is another angelfish mutation. Of three different gold angelfish mutations since the 1950s, the only one still around is "new gold." It's located at the same locus as the dark gene (D) and therefore is an allele. It is recessive to (masked by) both the wild-type and the dark gene and so we symbolize it as d^g. Its phenotype can only occur when its genotype is homozygous $d^g d^g$. It will be masked in heterozygotes whether they are wild-type or dark fish (d^g + or Dd^g), the first resembling the wild (silver) angelfish and the second appearing as a dark angel.

Dark color, D, is an incompletely dominant gene, as it only partially masks the color of the normal (wild) angelfish. We could set up the same Punnet Square, using D for dark and + for the wild-type (silver) body color with black stripes, and get another kind of result.

Zebra lace raised under continuous light.

Leopard angelfish.

Blushing half-black angelfish.

The half-black angelfish must be raised with extensive water changes.

Pearly or pearlscale angelfish.

Blushing gold marble with half-black body.

Zebra lace angelfish raised under continuous light.

Hormone-induced "green" angelfish produced in Bangkok.

The phenotype of an angelfish is what it looks like based on its genes (genotype) plus environmental influences. As an example of environmental effects, silver angelfish raised in constant light grow up without dark bars on the body and appear silvery, while those raised under ordinary conditions of 14 hours of light have dark bars on the body. This reduced pigment, or silvery effect, can only develop early in life under prolonged photo-periods, and is irreversible.

In this case, having the dark gene from only one parent (D+) would result in a partially dark angelfish called "black lace," while a pair of dark genes (DD) would result in a black angelfish. Almost all dark pigment mutations in angelfish are caused by genes with incomplete dominance, so that a homozygote is more intensely pigmented (or unpigmented) than the heterozygote.

The eight or so black pigment mutant genes are divided into at least two groups of alleles. Any gene from one group will be inherited independently from any gene in the other group. As an example, there is another angelfish mutant called stripeless. Although both the dark gene and the stripeless gene affect coloration, they do so independently, and so they must occur in different locations on the chromosomes. These different loci (short for chromosome locations) mean they are not alleles.

If we crossed a black angel with an extra-longfinned silver angel, all the offspring would be black lace and longfinned because both D and V are dominant genes. D and V are not alleles to each other because they do not occupy comparable loci on a pair of chromosomes.

You could use the Punnet Square to predict ratios for any other characteristic controlled by a single gene. The parental fish could be brother and sister, father and daughter, mother and son, cousins, or unrelated. What matters is whether the traits are controlled by a single pair of genes (alleles), whether the genes are dominant or recessive, or whether they are unrelated so that you could have both colors passed on and combined in the offspring.

You can handle two non-allelic genes at a time using Punnet Squares, and even more when you become comfortable with the technique. We know longfin is incompletely dominant to normal, and albino is recessive to wild-type. What happens when you cross an albino veiltail with a carrier of albino having extra-long fins?

(albino veiltail male)

		Va	+a
(female carrier of albino with extra-long fins)	Va	VVaa	V+aa
	V+	VVa+	V+a+

One quarter will be extra-longfinned albinos (VVaa), one quarter will be extra-longfinned silvers carrying the albino gene (VVa+), one quarter will be longfinned albinos (V+aa), and one quarter will be longfinned silvers carrying the albino gene (V+a+).

CHECKLIST

Genetics: A Brief Recap

Genetics is the study of hereditary traits. Since angelfish traits are controlled by genes, you need to keep the following concepts in mind when considering their traits:

1 All chromosomes occur in pairs; one of each pair is contributed by the mother and the other by the father.

2 Mitosis differs from meiosis in that cells are divided during mitosis, with each pair of chromosomes duplicating themselves. During meiosis, however, each egg or sperm cell gets only one member of a chromosome pair from each parent.

3 When the sperm cell fertilizes the egg, a new individual called a zygote is created. This individual's cells begin the process of mitosis.

4 A gene is dominant or recessive depending on whether it "masks" (dominates) another gene or is masked by (becomes recessive to) another gene.

5 Alleles refers to two different genes that occupy the same position on chromosome pairs and affect the same trait.

6 Diploid refers to paired chromosomes. It is denoted as $2n$.

7 Haploid refers to unpaired chromosomes in sperm or egg cells. It is symbolized as n.

8 Punnet squares are used to calculate the odds of each type of sperm cell allele combining with each type of egg cell allele.

9 Genotype is the genetic makeup of a cell.

10 Phenotype refers to the appearance of an individual.

FANCY STRAINS OF ANGELFISH

Angelfish strains differ in color and finnage, in the genes responsible for those traits, and in environmental or developmental changes as the fish grow to adulthood. The names of angelfish strains can be confusing and the ways of producing or maintaining fancy strains even more so.

In this chapter we'll review the principal strains of fancy angelfish, and provide tips on how to keep those strains going in your own aquariums.

Mutations

Mutations can be dominant (capital letter) or recessive (small letter) to wild-type (+). Many angelfish genes are for incomplete dominance (blending). Put another way, an angelfish with two incomplete dominance genes for a trait (homozygous) has a double dose of the gene and therefore a double dose of the trait. There are exceptions, but incomplete dominant genes yielding single dose and double dose phenotypes are a recurring phenomenon through many angelfish mutations.

All specific mutations at a specific location on a specific chromosome (locus) are alleles of

Homozygous marble angelfish.

one another. For any pair of chromosomes you cannot have more than one pair of alleles no matter how many exist in the population. Imagine, for example, that a fish could be green, purple, red, blue, or orange, but that the genes for these colors were all on exactly the same locus, and that fin length was on another locus. You might also have fish with three colors at one locus and four other colors at another locus. In this case, you could get two colors on the same fish, since colors at different loci don't interfere with each other. Genes that occur at the same locus are called alleles.

Dr. Joanne Norton singlehandedly worked out the genetics of virtually every strain of angelfish, and the origins of strains produced by chemical and environmental manipulations. A glance at the reference list will reveal that this chapter would not be possible without her contributions. For more on angelfish genetics and fish genetics in particular, see Norton (1982).

In angelfish, there are at least four different mutant loci for color patterns, one for fin length, and one for scale type. At each of the color pattern loci, there may be one or more different alleles. One group of alleles is small, consisting only of the gene for long fins (V).

Veiltail: The gene for long fins is an incomplete dominant written V. An angelfish carrying the gene can be VV (homozygous) or $V+$ (heterozygous). The common heterozygous longfin angelfish ($V+$) has fins much enlarged compared with the wild-type ($++$), yet shorter than the homozygous veiltail angelfish (VV), which can also be thought of as the extra-longfinned angelfish. Veiltails (VV) produce only veiltail offspring (VV), whereas longfins ($V+$) produce offspring that are normal finned ($++$), longfinned ($V+$), and veiltails (VV). A wild-type fish crossed with a longfinned type will produce both longfins and wild-types. Use a Punnet Square to predict ratios from any combination of genes for fin length (V and $+$).

Another group of alleles (genes occupying the same locus) consists of the genes for dark pigment (D), marble (D^m), and new gold (D^g).

Black lace and black: The dark gene (D) is an incomplete dominant for extended dark pigment diffused over the body in areas normally silvery. A single dose (heterozygous or $D+$) results in a dark gray fish with the black stripes still prominent, called black lace. A double dose (homozygous or DD) results in a deep black angelfish with the stripes almost obscured by the diffused black pigment. Black angelfish are weaker than black lace, the fry with higher mortality and slower growth rates.

Marble: Marble angelfish have black areas disrupted into broken lines and blotches. The gene for marble is an allele of the gene for dark, i.e., they occur in the same position on the chromosomes. That means a fish can have one or the other gene on each of its chromosomes, but not both. Because marble is an allele of dark, it is written D^m. D^m is an incomplete dominant, with the heterozygous (D^m+) producing a strikingly contrasting fish with a light marble pattern, and the double dose homozygous condition (D^mD^m) producing a fish with so much dark pigment as to appear blotched or dark marble. The heterozygous light marble (D^m+) has the more contrasting, striking, and appealing pattern, and is as vigorous as wild angelfish. Homozygotes, or dark marbles, are weak and slow growing, with higher mortality rates comparable to homozygous black angels.

New gold: There is only one kind of gold angelfish in the hobby today, but because it is the third one reported (the other two have all but disappeared), it is called new gold. The new gold gene is an allele of dark, and is recessive to that gene. For precision (as there may be other recessive genes to be discovered), it is written d^g, with the first letter indicating its recessiveness to dark and the superscript denoting the new gold characteristic. As you might expect, the homozygous recessive fish (d^gd^g) breeds true with 100 percent new gold offspring.

Best commercial darks and marbles: There are three possible genotypes for marble angelfish, D^mD^m, D^m+, and D^md^g. For the most attractive and vigorous marbles, Norton recommended crossing D^mD^m with silver ($++$) to produce 100 percent D^m+ high contrast light marbles, or crossing D^mD^m dark marbles with d^g, resulting in 100 percent jet black marbles. Norton pointed out that d^g somehow enhances the intensity of blackness in both D^m and D angels.

Other non-allelic golds: The first gold angelfish in the hobby was called Naja Gold, and the location of the mutant gene (locus) and its possible allelic relationships to other pigment genes remains a mystery. This fish when young looks like any silver angelfish, but at about nine months begins losing black pigment above, replacing it with gold, and then developing black pigment below, followed by a loss of that pigment to more gold. During development of the gold color, the fish is variously pied black, silver, and gold and more attractive than the final gold stage. Naja Golds are rare today.

A second early gold strain was called Hong Kong Gold. That mutation occurred on a locus different from all other known pigment mutations and was recessive to wild-type. The gene is symbolized *hg*, so a heterozygous fish was a carrier (+*hg*) that showed no gold at all, but a homozygous (*hghg*) would be a gold fish that yielded 100 percent gold offspring.

Smokey and chocolate: Smokey angelfish have a marblelike splotch of black pigment in the rear half of the otherwise silvery body, concentrations of black pigment at the tips of the dorsal and anal fins and on the jaws, and an almost all-black tail fin. Chocolate angelfish are darker with an expanded blotching over almost all the flank, but differ from marble in their characteristic black tails and jaws. The smokey gene (*Sm*) is an incomplete dominant producing smokey when heterozygous (*Sm*+), and chocolate when homozygous (*SmSm*). Smokey and chocolate occupy a unique locus and are not alleles of other known mutant genes.

Two extreme mutations, one causing doubling of the stripes and the other resulting in loss of stripes, occur at the same locus and are alleles.

Ghost and blushing: An incomplete dominant gene, stripeless (*S*) as a heterozygote (*S*+), produces a ghost angel, a fish without dark body stripes, but with one or two black blotches or ovals at most (sometimes not even that). The homozygous form (*SS*) eliminates the iridophores on the gill covers, eliminating opacity in juveniles. The remaining translucence reveals the red gill filaments below. This almost pigmentless, reduced iridophore angelfish strain is called blushing. It differs from all other mutations in that the double dose affects two different systems (melanin pigment stripes and patches on the body of adults and guanine crystal iridocytes on the opercles). As in black and marble, the homozygous form is less vigorous than the heterozygous. Additionally, the *SS* form is unusually susceptible to microbial infections that cause erosion of the gills and fins. Other reported problems with blushing fry are small size and high mortality from swim bladder infections.

Zebra: Normal silver angelfish have one prominent dark stripe through the eye and two on the body, plus about eight stripes in the fins. Zebra angelfish have two additional body stripes (only the rear one prominent), about 50 percent more dark bands in the fins, and are generally darker bodied than silver or wild angelfish. Zebra is an allele of stripeless, meaning that it occurs at the same location on the chromosome as the *S* gene. For that reason, it is designated with the symbol S^z. Unlike stripeless, zebra is a simple dominant, with both the heterozygous (S^z+) and homozygous (S^zS^z) similar in appearance. Crossing S^zS^z to ++ yields all S^z+ offspring, and crossing those offspring to one another yields 75 percent zebra and 25 percent silver, consistent with a simple

Top left: Marble smokey veiltail angelfish.
Middle left: Hong Kong Gold, homozygous veiltail.
Bottom left: Naja Gold is seldom seen today.
Top right: New Gold angelfish, heterozygous for the longfin gene.
Bottom right: New Gold fed on a diet of frozen krill.

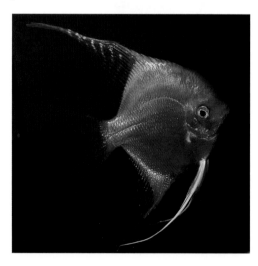

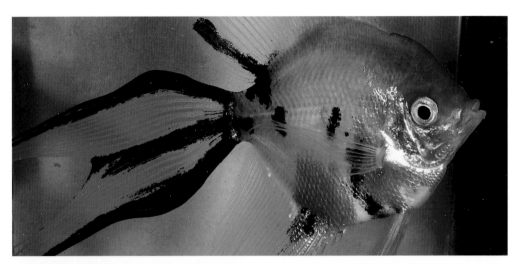

Top: Gold marble blushing veiltail angelfish.
Above: Juvenile blushing smokey angelfish.
Above left: Blushing angelfish, lacking
pigment and quanine.
Left: Naja Gold angelfish in intermediate
color phase.

dominant. Young homozygotes are much smaller than heterozygotes.

Half black: In half-black angelfish the rear stripe darkens followed by the entire rear third to half of the body, while the front remains normal. The gene for half black is recessive to wild-type, and not allelic to any other known angelfish gene. In this discussion, we will call half black *hb*. A heterozygous fish appears normal (*hb+*), but a homozygous individual (*hbhb*) will be genotypically half black. The phenotypic expression of half black is environmentally induced or, more to the point, its expression can be environmentally blocked.

To get half-black offspring from phenotypically half-black adults, feed them well and provide massive, frequent water changes during the first weeks and months of life. Failure to change water, failure to provide excellent nutrition (massive frequent feedings of *Artemia*), and failure to provide growing space (keeping the fish crowded) can all prevent the expression of half black even in homozygous half-black fish. This prevention of expression is reversible, and providing better conditions later in life can bring out the half-black pattern. A partial pattern develops in fish that do not get excellent care.

Pearly: A unique mutation manifested in the skin, and known as pearly or crystal, is the result of a simple recessive gene, which we'll refer to here as *p*. It controls the appearance of imbedded scales in the skin to create a wavy body surface that reflects light from any angle, producing a glistening angelfish. Pearly breeds true when homozygous (*pp*), but yields all wild-type in the heterozygous offspring (*p+*) of pearly (*pp*) times wild-type (*++*). Brother to sister matings of the normal looking heterozy-

gotes (*p+*) yield 25 percent pearly (*pp*), as expected with a simple recessive gene.

Interactions

Genes sometimes interact with unpredictable consequences. As described under marbles, $d^{ng}+$ enhances both D and D^m to increase black pigmentation. These are all alleles.

A cross based on interacting non-allelic genes was the origin of Black Velvet. Here, the gene for blushing, or homozygous stripeless angelfish (*SS*), was combined with the most intensely black of the dark gene strains (Dd^g), yielding an intensely black angelfish.

Epistasis: This is the action of one gene affecting the expression of an entirely different (non-allelic) gene. For example, homozygous new gold ($d^g d^g$), which is an allele of the dark gene (*D*), prevents the expression of zebra (S^z), smokey (*Sm*), and half black (*hb*), all non-alleles of dark. The dark gene for marble (D^m) is epistatic to the gene for zebra (S^z), almost completely preventing its expression.

Induced Phenotypes

Green: This is a fake phenotype because there is no green gene. Wild angelfish from Guyana sometimes have a tint of green or blue on the head, but so far there has never been a green angel based on a mutant gene. Green angels in the trade are ordinary angelfish treated by unscrupulous producers with methyl testosterone, a synthetic male hormone added to the water to enhance colors. Unless the drug is continually added to the water or the diet, the green color fades. These fish may be reproductively damaged, resulting in fewer and weaker fry than normal fish. The green color is not genetic, not passed to the offspring, and not permanent.

Reduced pattern: Angelfish raised with 12 to 14 hours of light alternating with a period of darkness develop normal stripes. Wild-type angelfish raised in continuous light do not develop stripes. Zebra angelfish raised in continuous light develop black spots, but not stripes. Black lace angelfish raised in continuous light are dusky, but without stripes. Solid black angelfish raised in continuous light also fail to develop stripes, resulting in a velvety black (and attractive) fish. Stripeless angelfish raised in continuous light may not show the oval blotch (a reduced stripe). These effects are induced only in early stage angelfish raised under these conditions, and the effects are not reversible. This effect is developmental, and not inherited.

Marble angelfish (at least some types) and smokey angelfish do not show effects from being raised under continuous light. Presumably only stripes are susceptible to alteration, but not other manifestations of melanin pigmentation.

Wild angelfish imported from at least Guyana and Peru (and probably elsewhere) vary in stripe density, some with strong striping and some silver and stripeless. It was long thought that placing silver fish on a dark background would bring out the stripes that were faded by a bright background. That is not true. The silvery or stripeless fish never develop stripes. Is there a relationship between the light effect in captive fish and variation in wild fish? Perhaps stripeless or silver wild fish were spawned in the open during the long days of summer, while normal striped fish were spawned in cooler months and/or in densely shaded nesting sites.

The cobra angelfish is not a distinct genetic type, but a faded fish resulting from breeding fish with both the zebra (S^z) and dark genes (D), and raising them in continuous light.

DISEASES

Fish are armed to resist invaders. Still, invaders find ways to attack a weakened or wounded fish, and even healthy fish may succumb to overwhelming numbers of invaders that, in small doses, could be resisted.

The Host–Parasite Relationship

It's as normal for a wild fish to have parasites as it is a forest to have trees. In nature, the parasite burden is seldom overwhelming, and the fish and its parasites appear to get along famously; the infections are subclinical (no symptoms). The relationship between the host fish and its parasites has developed over millennia. Parasites that were overly damaging managed to kill off their hosts and their own opportunities to leave offspring. What remains today is a harmonized ecosystem of host fish and a myriad of parasites on and inside the body.

How do the offspring of parasites reach new hosts to carry on the next generation? That's complicated, but the most frequent problem is that the hosts are few and far between. The low likelihood of a baby parasite finding a host is offset by an increase in numbers of offspring. That's the way to assure that the next generation of parasites will be successful.

Zebra lace angelfish with abnormal pigment pattern.

In the past and in the wild, if too many parasites were produced, they might overwhelm the host and kill it and, ergo, themselves. If too few offspring were produced, there might not be a successful new generation of parasites and, voilà (as opposed to ergo), the parasites again disappeared. It's clear that the production of parasites is delicately balanced against the size of the host population.

We've seen time and again that when hosts become unusually abundant, they often suffer an epidemic of disease that wipes out much of the population. It's a natural balance of nature. If too many parasites are produced on too many hosts, and those hosts are now crowded, then the odds are that the hosts will suffer from an overwhelming infection rate. And when the parasites are too demanding (because they are too numerous), the host suffers and sometimes dies.

Pathology

Pathology is the study of disease processes. Wild fish are vulnerable to poor water quality (low pH, high heat, low dissolved oxygen,

TIP

Testing Wild Fish as Carriers of Viral or Bacterial Diseases

Gratzek et al. (1992) recommended a way for aquarists to test whether wild fish were carriers of pathogenic viruses or other microbes. Disease-free fry of domestic angelfish are added to the water of newly imported angelfish in quarantine. If the domestic fry quickly become sick and die, you can presume the wild fish are symptomless carriers of a pathogenic microbe (virus or bacterium).

leaching of natural chemicals from the ground or from toxic plants) and from overwhelming infections of parasites. Any of these organisms or conditions might damage certain cells that are part of organs necessary for life.

We can see some types of damage such as bubbles in the fins, air bubbles in the eyes, abnormal swelling of the body to the extent the scales point outward, raw bloody sores, ragged fins trailing mucus, or pimples on the body. Under the microscope we can see other pathologic responses such as proliferation of epithelial cells in the gills (hyperplasia) and enlargement of epithelial and mucus cells (hypertrophy). Any pathologic change can lead to further degradation in the ability of the fish to feed, grow, breathe, reproduce, or even to survive to the next day. If the inducer of environmentally induced pathology (toxins, low pH) is not removed by, for example, a water change, then the pathology increases and the

fish deteriorates. Starving fishes, or fishes with dietary deficiencies, may become thin, with skeletal features showing through the skin, especially about the head; starving or dietary deficient fish often have lipid (fat) deposits in the liver. If pathology is caused by a parasite, the fish might deteriorate and die, or marshall its immune resources and recover.

Immunity

The epidermis and dermis make up the skin, a highly refractory barrier to parasitic protozoa and bacteria. The dermis anchors the scales, refractory to penetrating parasites and to debris against which the fish may brush while foraging or fleeing predators. Yet additional protection is afforded by antimicrobial mucus emitted by specialized cells in the epithelium of the gills and skin.

Recovery from the pathology of disease may occur when the fish's defenses kick in and limit the success of the multiplying or growing parasite, eventually walling off or disposing of the parasite. Many of the defenses are located in the bloodstream, blood vessels, and specialized organs such as the liver. These defenses are both cellular and chemical. They are based on a dozen kinds of white blood cells. Some engulf the invaders and digest them (phagocytes). Others (T-cells and B-cells) release substances (antibodies) that coat the invader to make it easier for other white cells to recognize, attack, and kill it. Still others release digestive or killing fluids (cytokinins) to liquify the invader. The range of weaponry of the fish's body is amazing, and some of these defenses become stronger if the fish is attacked by the same kind of parasite later in life.

Unlike the skin and phagocytes, initiation of the antibody-based immune system depends

Major Groups of Bacteria

Group 1.	Spiral Bacteria or Spirochetes
Group 2.	Motile Aerobic or Microaerophilic, Gram-Negative Spirals or Curved Rods
Group 3.	Usually Nonmotile Gram-Negative Curved Rods
Group 4.	Aerobic/Microaerophilic Gram-Negative Rods and Cocci
Group 5.	Facultatively Anaerobic Gram-Negative Rods
Group 6.	Gram-Negative, Anaerobic, Straight, Curved, or Spiral Bacteria
Group 7.	Sulfur Reducing Bacteria
Group 8.	Anaerobic Gram-Negative Cocci
Group 9.	Rickettsias and Chlamydias
Group 10.	Anaerobic Photosynthesizers
Group 11.	Aerobic Photosynthesizers
Group 12.	Sulfur, Manganese, Iron, Ammonia, and Nitrite Oxidizing Bacteria
Group 13.	Budding and Branched Bacteria
Group 14.	Encased Bacteria
Group 15.	Nonphotosynthetic, Nonfruiting, Gliding Bacteria
Group 16.	Fruiting, Gliding Myxobacteria
Group 17.	Gram-Positive Cocci
Group 18.	Sporeforming Gram-Positive Rods and Cocci
Group 19.	Regular Nonsporeforming Gram-Positive Rods
Group 20.	Irregular Nonsporeforming Gram-Positive Rods
Group 21.	Mycobacteria (Acid-Fast Bacteria)
Groups 22–29.	Actinomycetes (Fungus-Like Bacteria)
Group 30.	Mycoplasmas (Modern Bacteria without Cell Walls)
Group 31.	Methane-Producing Bacteria
Group 32.	Ancient Sulfate Reducing Bacteria
Group 33.	Halobacteria (Salt Bacteria)
Group 34.	Ancient Bacteria without Cell Walls
Group 35.	Hot Vent Sulfur Bacteria

on temperature and in some cases exposure to metals. At low temperature, the defenses may not work, or the antiparasite chemicals (cytokines) may not be manufactured or secreted by the fish. For that reason, chilled fish may succumb to disease agents that warm fish could readily resist. Copper may damage the immune system, and the use of this medicament should be a last resort.

Noninfectious Pathology

Light: Suddenly turning on a bright light can send fish thrashing in panic against glass, rocks, and even out of the aquarium. The effect of light is even more dramatic when wild fish, packed in darkness for 24 to 48 hours, are suddenly exposed to bright light during unpacking. The fish's muscles go into tetanus, with fins erect and gills flared and immovable, the body trembling and then still. With muscles unable to function, ventilation freezes to a stop and the fish suffocates. Few fish recover from light shock. The condition is not treatable, but it is avoidable. Always unpack fish (especially wild) in dim light or semi-darkness, and maintain them under low light conditions for at least 24 hours.

Temperature and oxygen: Cold water can weaken a fish's immune system and even

Many parasites and other conditions can only be diagnosed with the aid of a microscope.

prevent it from mounting an antibody response. High heat can deplete water of dissolved oxygen while increasing the fish's need for respiratory oxygen. For these reasons, aeration and warmth support healthy angelfishes.

Chlorine and chloramine: No chemicals kill more aquarium fishes than chlorine and chloramine. Both are widely used disinfectants in municipal tap water. The chlorination byproduct—hypochlorite—oxidizes substances at the cell surface of the gills, leading to loss of cellular potassium and swelling of the cells as fluids rush inside. Because of the damaged membranes and loss of ions, the fish cannot maintain blood pH and it dies of acidosis. Chlorine levels of 0.1 mg/L in waters with low organic loads are acutely fatal to fish.

pH and hardness: Wild angelfishes (all species) are found in quiet, soft, slightly acidic, tannin-stained water. Reports of angels from "white" water do not indicate riffles or rapids, but rather silt-laden, opaque water and may represent observations following heavy rains and silt-laden runoff from disturbed land. Wild angelfishes do not tolerate sudden elevations in pH and should not be exposed to water above pH 6.8, whereas domestic angelfishes readily tolerate pH values close to 8.0. Wild angelfishes deteriorate in hard water, suggesting a low number of chloride cells in their gill tissues and an inability to maintain salt balance. Domestic strains thrive in hard water, and may have adapted by increased concentrations of chloride cells.

Carbon dioxide: The most important waste products of metabolism are carbon dioxide and ammonia. At neutral pH, carbon dioxide is in equilibrium with carbonic acid (carbonate) and bicarbonate (common buffers). Excess carbon dioxide is taken up by plants or diffuses into the atmosphere. When fish are sealed (as in plastic shipping bags), the excess carbon dioxide cannot escape and reaches higher and higher concentrations that are at first anesthetic and finally toxic. In fact, fish locked into plastic bags for protracted periods seldom die of lack of oxygen, but rather of carbon dioxide toxicity, which shuts down breathing.

Ammonia and nitrite: Ammonia, a product of nitrogen metabolism (degradation of proteins and nucleic acids) is toxic at only 0.02 ppm (two hundredths of a milligram in a liter of water). In natural systems and in aged aquariums with rocks, gravel, or other extensive surface areas (as within a filter), the surfaces become coated with aerobic bacteria that use ammonia and convert it to less toxic nitrite. With time and sufficient production of ammonia, there develops a large population of ammonia-using bacteria that can respond rapidly to sudden surges in ammonia concentration, as occurs when a fish dies or excess uneaten food is attacked by decomposition bacteria and fungi. As even nitrite is toxic, it must be removed and, in aquaria, another group of bacteria is encouraged to expand its populations (bloom) when the nitrite concentration increases. These bacteria use nitrite and convert it to a nontoxic waste product, nitrate.

Nitrate: Although it is nontoxic, it is a growth-inhibiting substance. It can be used by plants (or algae), but often stimulates a bloom of "blue-green algae" called cyanobacteria. These slimy microbes emit noxious cyanotoxins that give the water a medicine odor and weaken fish that then succumb to invasive microbes or die directly from intoxication. Cyanobacteria can sometimes be eliminated

Marble from gold marble.

with erythromycin, but the drug also kills beneficial nitrogen cycle bacteria. Removal of nitrates can be partially accomplished by duckweed or other green plants, but mostly by water changes. There is no filter or equipment available today that can be relied on to remove nitrates, and water changes remain the single most effective method of maintaining high-quality water. Lowering nitrates through water changes is as important as a balanced diet in optimizing growth.

Nutritional deficiency: Some strains of black angelfish have high infant mortality rates. Substantial losses occur even after the fry commence feeding on *Artemia* nauplii, and continue despite heavy feeding of this nutritious food. The amino acid alanine is used to make the black pigment melanin, but alanine is also needed for neurological and excretory system development. Enriching the diet with highly unsaturated fatty acids (as in cod liver oil), essential to neurological development, enhances survival and growth, perhaps by assisting the young to use their limited dietary alanine more efficiently.

Metals: Copper damages the immune system, suggesting that other metals might have similar effects. Young angelfish treated with copper sulfate solution to eliminate parasites may subsequently succumb to microbes that copper-free angelfish regularly resist.

Gas bubble disease: Protrusion of the eyes caused by gas bubble disease can be confirmed by finding blood at the base of the eye or bubbles adjacent to hemorrhages in the fin membranes. Gas bubble disease results from water supersaturated with air as a result of sudden warming of cold water, suddenly reduced pressure (from the high pressure tap), or venturi absorption of air through a powerhead.

Hole-in-the-head disease: Erosion of the nostrils and the lateral line pores of the body and, especially, the head is not associated with any infectious disease, but appears to be a nonspecific response to irritation. The causes are probably high concentrations of nitrates or cyanotoxins. Hole-in-the-head does not occur in tanks provided with regular massive water changes. The scarring is irreversible.

Infectious Diseases

"Angelfish plague" and "angelfish AIDS" do not exist. These are names invented by importers and wholesalers for disease outbreaks that did not respond to their normal handling and treatment. Reported symptoms varied from sliming, to eroding lesions, swelling, and hanging head-up or head-down in a corner. These outbreaks are caused by a variety of mostly bacterial diseases that got their foothold because of stress resulting from sudden changes in water quality or deteriorating water quality. The most frequent causes of these outbreaks have included the bacteria *Flexibacter, Pseudomonas, Mycobacterium,* and other species, plus *Chilodonella* and other protozoans. The disease agents may be susceptible to certain antibiotics and antimicrobials if the drugs are delivered at an early stage of disease, at an effective dose, and through an effective route (such as food, bath, and so on, depending on the microbe and medicament).

Viruses

Viruses occur in wild fishes of many kinds and can be transmitted in aquariums, ponds, or at a dealer's facility from symptomless or even unrelated fishes. In the laboratory they are detected by damaged cell cultures in petri dishes (the cytopathic effect or CPE) or by actually seeing the arrays of particles (virions) with an electron microscope.

TIP

Avoiding Parasites and Diseases in Community Tanks

You can most efficiently avoid parasites and diseases by avoiding incidental and intermediate hosts, such as pond-grown and wild fishes (flagellated and ciliated protozoans), snails (for digenetic trematodes), copepods (for nematodes and thorny-headed worms), and not using sick fish as food for larger healthy fish.

Most important, all new fish should be quarantined and observed for signs of disease for at least six weeks before placing them with your other community tank fishes.

Lymphocystis is an iridovirus infecting any marine or freshwater fish, and was reported in the Guatemalan *"Cichlasoma" synspilum*. The diagnostic strawberry eruptions on the body and fins consist of cells enlarged many times their normal diameter (cytomegaly) because of the viruses inside. The infection is occasionally fatal, but in many fishes the lesions resorb in a few weeks.

Systemic iridovirus infection in angelfish is caused by a more important related virus characterized by cytomegaly that does kill the infected cells (Rodger et al. 1997). The six-sided viral particles invade the kidney (leading to ascites or swelling), the blood vessels behind the eyes (leading to exophthalmia or pop-eye), and other parts of the body. The mortality was reported to be 70 percent and there is no treatment.

Infectious pancreatic necrosis (IPN) is a fatal virus infecting tropical fish at least under laboratory conditions.

Several viruses occurring naturally in angelfish were not proven to be associated with disease (Gratzek et al. 1992). However, it's possible they could produce disease in stressed fish, but tests haven't been conducted (Gratzek, personal communication).

There are no treatments for fish virus diseases. The correct approach is to destroy contaminated fish, sterilize tanks, nets, and instruments with chlorine bleach, and avoid transmitting contaminated water with your hands or nets. Ultraviolet disinfection has been successful in reducing the numbers of viruses and bacteria in large breeding facilities.

Bacterial Diseases

Few bacteria cause disease. Most of them have more important things to do (see box on

TIP

Best Treatment for Sick Fish
Always remove sick fish to quarantine for treatment with appropriate medicaments and heat. Professional breeders often dispose of sick fish rather than treat them in order to rapidly eliminate the disease agent from the premises.

page 59). For those that cause disease in fishes, we have a few tricks of our own.

Of the medicaments effective against bacterial diseases, those synthesized in the laboratory, such as sulfa drugs, are called antimicrobials. Chemicals produced by bacteria or fungi are called antibiotics. Examples are penicillin from *Penicillium* and streptomycin from *Streptomyces*.

Almost all disease-causing bacteria of tropical fishes are gram-negative, which means they become colored pink or red with the gram staining procedure. Gram-positive bacteria, such as those responsible for the nitrogen cycle, are dyed purple by this procedure. They dye differently because gram-negative and gram-positive bacteria have different chemical forms of cell wall structure. The importance is that certain drugs interfere with synthesis of gram-negative or gram-positive cell walls, but not both. And so drugs such as penicillin, erythromycin, or streptomycin—while effective in eliminating gram-positive bacteria such as *Renibacterium* by interfering with production of new cell walls—are generally ineffective on gram-negative bacteria such as *Aeromonas*, *Pseudomonas*,

Above: The raspberry-like lesions of lymphocystis show up distinctly in this marine angelfish.

Right: Cotton wool disease shows clearly in this fancy betta, and it can kill in 24 hours.

and *Flexibacter* (*Cytophaga*). Broad spectrum antibiotics, and many antimicrobials, are effective on both kinds of bacteria.

The furans are important water-soluble antimicrobials for treating gram-negative bacterial diseases. Nifurpirinol (furanace, furazolidone) is rapidly absorbed from water and used as a bath. A single dose of 2 mg/gallon (0.5 mg/L) for six hours may be sufficient. Treat in dim light or darkness, as it degrades in bright light.

The quinolones (oxolinic acid derivatives) are broad spectrum antibiotics effective against gram-positive and gram-negative bacteria and can be added to water or food, or injected in large fish. They must be used in a bare quarantine tank because they can also kill nitrogen cycle bacteria in gravel and filters.

Enrofloxacin is a broad spectrum drug that kills bacteria in blood and inside fish cells at low concentrations, and is nontoxic to fish.

Many other over-the-counter medicaments sold in pet stores are poorly absorbed from water, must be presented in food or injected into the body, and are not suitable for aquarium use by the general public. If furans or quinolones do not produce desired results, take a group of sick fish to a veterinarian for a presumptive diagnosis and prescription medicament.

Cotton wool disease is an infection of the epithelium produced by the gram-negative *Flexibacter (Cytophaga) columnaris* and its relatives. They usually cause disease in newly arrived shipments of wild or domestic fish subjected to low temperature, depressed water quality, low oxygen concentrations, or crowding. It begins as a translucent layer on the skin that rapidly expands, eating away the flesh. The edges of the lesion are often bloody. An exudate, or pus, then leaches into the water column. That exudate is a solid mass of filamentous bacteria multiplying so fast that they

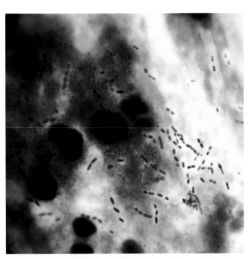

Mycobacteria appear as red sticks under the acid-fast procedure.

Gram-negative bacteria in the bloodstream can cause swelling as a result of fluid retention.

spread out of the fish and into the water. The same growth occurs simultaneously inside the fish, and death typically occurs in 12 to 24 hours from the first sign of the disease. Discard all fish with advanced lesions. Fish with early stage lesions should be quarantined and treated with four teaspoons of marine salt to the gallon, and potassium chromate, or potassium permanganate, according to package directions.

Vibrios, genus *Vibrio*, are susceptible to gram-negative antibiotics, but the fish must be treated promptly. Bloody lesions, pop-eye (exophthalmia), and protruding intestines are frequent signs of disease. Vibrios attack and kill rapidly, necessitating destruction of advanced cases in addition to treating symptomless fish with which they are in contact.

Mycobacteria are the Acid Fast bacteria, a name based on a staining procedure that detects bacteria with waxy walls, rendering

them refractory to most antibiotics. Many *Mycobacterium* species grow slowly so the medicaments take a long time to have an effect. The common mycobacterial infections of fishes are associated with impaired immune systems that result from stress or old age. The disease manifests as swelling and loss of color, or as bloody lesions anywhere on the body. The organs are filled with granulomas, or walled off aggregations of live and dead white blood cells, surrounding clumps of bacteria. There are no cost-effective treatments of this contagious "fish TB" disease.

Other gram-negative bacteria can be secondary invaders of wounds or lesions in stressed fish. Symptoms include gasping at the surface, failure to eat, wasting away, light blotches in the skin, and swelling with protruding scales. Quinolones and furans are effective during early stages of diseases, but not after the bacteria have expanded into the

Copper Sulfate

Copper sulfate at 0.2 parts per million (ppm) is effective at neutral pH, but precipitates at elevated pH. At low pH, the precipitate comes out of solution. If copper treatment has been used repeatedly in the same aquarium, the sediments may contain a considerable quantity of precipitate. Should the pH be depressed (adjusted) in this tank, the solubilized copper from the sediments may reach lethal concentrations. Copper is not an appropriate treatment for wild angelfish that require soft acid water. Copper should only be used in well-buffered, neutral water of moderate hardness. Its concentration is difficult to control in soft acidic water. Copper depresses the immune system in fishes.

bloodstream (septicemia) or kidneys, leading to osmotic imbalance and the accumulation of nitrogenous wastes and fluids in the blood (visualized by swelling with scale protrusion). Infectious pop-eye results from gas production by bacteria invading the bloodstream (septicemia), and is usually terminal.

Protozoan Diseases

White spot disease: The most common disease of freshwater tropical fish is infection of the skin by *Ichthyophthirius multifilis*. The "ich" parasite is a ciliated protozoan, ubiquitous in water, that causes epidemics when fishes are stressed by cold temperatures or close contact with other heavily infected fish. Ich occurs in all aquariums and remains dormant until the fish are stressed or a new fish is introduced to the tank. Fish that recover from ich seldom become seriously infested again, but can be carriers.

A few small white spots appear and several days later their number and the size increase dramatically. In the ich life cycle, a young protozoan penetrates the skin and grows to a large size—the white spot—that can attain the size of a pinhead. At maturity, this trophont encysts and breaks out of the skin, falling to the bottom. The stage inside the cyst, called a tomont, divides into a thousand offspring. Then these infective theronts break out of the cyst to swim about seeking to infect more fish. Crowded fish are readily invaded. Once they burrow into the skin, they grow into trophonts and the cycle continues.

Parasites beneath the fish's skin or enclosed in a cyst are resistant to treatment. The free-swimming theronts, however, are susceptible to formalin, malachite green, or copper sulfate. Treatment consists of maintaining these chemicals in the water long enough for them to still be at high concentrations when the cysts hatch (follow package directions). Raise the temperature to quickly get to the theront stage and simultaneously boost the fishes' immune systems.

Other ciliates: (*Trichodina, Trichodinella, Chilodinella, Tetrahymena, Epistylis*) infect the skin or gills. They may be large enough to appear as small spots, or so small as to be invisible without recourse to viewing a skin scraping under a microscope. Symptoms include lethargy, eroding fins, scratching, hanging in a corner head up or down, or sudden dashing. Skin and gill protozoans are susceptible to 4 drops per gallon (4 L) of 100 percent formalin (37 percent formaldehyde) or a formalin-malachite green preparation, or to metronidazole. Diagnosis is with a smear of the skin (or swab of the gills) viewed under the microscope. A presumptive diagnosis can be made by placing uninfected fish in the same tank. If they develop symptoms within two days, an infectious protozoan agent is indicated.

Flagellates: *Ichthyobodo (=Costia)* are skin parasites and *Cryptobia* are gill parasites that proliferate when angelfish are maintained in crowded conditions. *Ichthyobodo* is an important angelfish parasite in hatcheries, causing mass mortalities. Slime production, difficulty breathing, and failure to eat are symptoms, but many fish show no symptoms before death. The fish should be treated with 100 percent formalin at 4 drops per gallon (4 L) of tank water, or with metronidazole.

Hexamita or *Spironucleus* is an intestinal parasite of wild angelfish, which under stressful conditions (crowding, poor feeding, chilling, association with diseased fishes), may overwhelm the host and interfere with absorption of nutrients. This flagellate may be a secondary invader of bacterial infections of the lateral line pores of the body and head.

Trypanoplasma is a blood parasite transmitted among wild fishes by leeches, and can only be diagnosed by a stained blood smear. Symptoms are lethargy and finally death. You can prevent its spread by removing any contact with blood-feeding leeches or blood-feeding branchiuran crustaceans (*Argulus*).

Velvet disease, caused by the photosynthetic dinoflagellate *Piscinoodinium*, causes mass mortalities of fry in dirty brood tanks and spreads through droplets in the air. Control is through darkness and cleanliness. In adult fish, the infection appears as a dusty golden layer on the body and eyes, and can be fatal if the lesions are secondarily invaded by bacteria. Adult fish can be treated with 0.1 to 0.2 ppm

copper sulfate. A salt (sea) water bath of 1 to 3 minutes, or until the fish show signs of distress, is also effective on domestic fish, but should not be applied to wild fish. Formalin is often effective, as is darkening the tank to deprive the parasites of the ability to photosynthesize.

Microsporida and myxosporida: *Henneguya, Glugea, Pleistophora, Cryptosporidium*, and other spore-forming protozoans live in deep tissues and internal organs where they are protected from medicaments. Many have complex life histories, some requiring more than one host for transmission. In general, they are untreatable and spread slowly but inexorably throughout the aquarium, and are readily transmitted—by water, cannibalism of dead fish, wet fish nets, gravel, hands, and perhaps even the air—to other aquaria. Symptoms include lumpy eruptions, discoloration (lightening) of the flesh throughout the body, with the fish becoming lethargic and seemingly stiff; translucent (low pigment) fish become opaque. Death is inevitable, and spores within the debris in the aquarium remain infective for weeks to years. Some of these organisms are moderately host-specific to one type of fish, but most are poorly known and their host ranges not determined. Infected fish should be destroyed and discarded (never fed to another fish), and the aquarium, its contents, and all nets and handling containers disinfected with household bleach in hot water.

Flatworms

The principal parasitic flatworms are tapeworms (cestodes), digenea (internal flukes), and monogenea (gill and skin flukes).

Monogenea are serious disease agents because they have a direct life cycle that can result in uncontrolled multiplication. Monogenea are of two general forms: those with tiny adhesive clamps and those with large suckers and anchors. Clamp-bearing monogenea usually occur on gills, whereas anchor-bearing monogenea occur on gills or skin, and are known even from the urinary bladders of tree frogs. These worms produce eggs or live offspring, and a single worm can produce many descendants to infect the same or adjacent fish. The parasites are introduced with infected (usually wild) fish, and spread especially when the worm is a fast-reproducing and non-host-specific type. *Gussevia spiralocirra* and *Sciadicleithrum iphthimum* occur in wild *Pterophyllum scalare* according to Thatcher (1991). Symptoms of monogenetic trematode infection in captivity include scratching, rapid breathing (gasping), and bloody lesions. Treat with 2 to 4 drops per gallon (4 L) of 37 to 40 percent formaldehyde (100 percent formalin), or

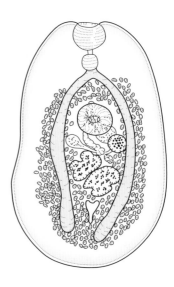

Crassicutis cichlasomae

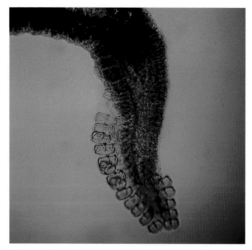

Clamp-bearing monogenetic trematodes occur only on the gills of fish.

immersion in marine water for five minutes or until the fish show signs of distress.

Digenea: Digenetic trematodes (digenea) are common in wild fish and can occur in any organ or tissue. Some digenea of South American cichlids include *Allocreadium* in the intestine and *Crassicutis* in the stomach. The life cycle of all digenea is indirect and requires a specific snail as an intermediate host. Many larval digenea in fish mature into adults when consumed by fish-eating birds. The birds then spread worm eggs in their own droppings. The eggs hatch in water into larvae that infect a snail in which they multiply and change into another larval form, that can once more infect a fish.

Wild and pond-reared angels with black spots, or white or yellow blobs in their skin, are carrying juveniles of digenetic trematodes that, outdoors, might have become adults had the fish been eaten by a bird. These juveniles ("yellow grubs") are unsightly, but do no harm.

Any fish covered in white spots or "grunge" might respond to a salt bath or to formalin treatment.

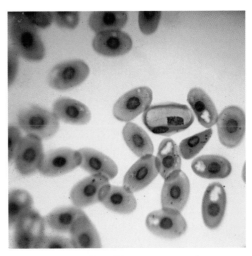

Protozoans such as **Haemoproteus** *live inside blood cells.*

The greatest killer of aquarium fish is chlorine in tap water.

Copepods are common in the gills of wild fish.

Adult digenea seldom cause disease. Digenea in the intestinal tract can be killed by the drug praziquantel at 2 mg/L, but those in other tissues (such as grubs) are not affected. In a review of Neotropical digenetic trematodes, Thatcher (1993) did not report any species from *Pterophyllum*, but it is not clear how many host fish, if any, were examined for members of this group.

Cestoda: Adult tapeworms occur in the intestine, but larvae might occur anywhere. Tapeworms require at least one intermediate host—and often two—to complete the life cycle, and cannot spread the infection from fish to fish. The first intermediate host is usually a copepod. Tapeworms are usually specific for the final host, but can use a variety of copepods. Even an infected wild fish shedding tapeworm eggs that are consumed by copepods in your aquarium is unlikely to spread the infection to other fishes because yet another host is probably required. Most importantly, tapeworms are generally harmless.

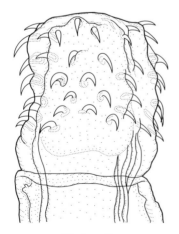

Pandosentis

An exception is *Bothriocephalus acheilognathus*, an Asian tapeworm introduced into American waters with grass carp, and apparently able to infect a wide range of copepods and fishes. It can infect pond-reared fish anywhere and is large enough to deform its host fish. Other species of *Bothriocephalus* and *Proteocephalus* from South American cichlids are innocuous. Tapeworms can be eliminated with praziquantel at 2 mg/L.

Roundworms

Nematode worms are common in wild fish and in pond culture, and usually spread by copepods. Nematodes coil like a watch spring, and are always narrow and cylindrical. They may be white, red, pink, peach, yellow, or brown, and often glisten. Some occur individually and do little or no harm, and others occur in massive infections that can burst the body wall. Some encyst (usually larval forms) and others wander through the body or a specific organ. *Capillaria pterophylli* is a common nematode in wild angelfishes that grazes on the intestinal lining and may cause massive infections. Larval and adult nematodes occur in pond-raised angelfishes and can spread among captive angelfishes fed *Daphnia* from outdoor ponds contaminated with copepods.

Treatment for nematodes is with thiabendazole, fenbendazole, or related nematocides in dog, cat, and horse deworming foods. Ask a veterinarian for any dewormer pet food except the heartworm medicine milbemycin, which is not effective against angelfish nematodes (Killino and Bodri, 1997).

Thorny-headed Worms

The Acanthocephala are dangerous worms

BREEDING PTEROPHYLLUM SCALARE

To breed angels, you can purchase a known breeding pair of almost any strain from your local aquarium store (usually on special order if somebody hasn't turned them in for credit), find them through magazine advertisements or at local aquarium societies, buy or bid for them at national shows and auctions, or raise your own from young. Most beginners and commercial breeders opt for the latter.

Getting Started

The techniques for breeding angelfish are different for the novice aquarist and the commercial breeder. Both, however, need to get a mated pair.

Angelfish do not breed at the drop of a hat with the first other angel to come along. They select their mates, a ritualized courtship establishing a relationship that includes protecting a territory. South American (as opposed to African) cichlids in general grow up before they consider sex with one another.

The odds of getting one male and one female from two fish are 50 percent. As you increase the number of fish, the odds of getting both sexes increase, so that with six fish, the odds become 95 percent that you'll get at least one of each sex rather than six of the same sex. If you purchase young angelfish, don't get just six

Angelfish eggs on a PVC pipe.

as some may die and others might be stunted or weak, and poor mates as adults. I like to start with a dozen fish, often dime-sized, as that is the youngest at which they are offered for sale, and they will never be less expensive. A fish twice that size is not much older and considerably more expensive. Go with the smallest fish, and get the most you can raise in a dedicated grow-out (not community) tank set aside just for this purpose.

Angelfish breed when approaching a year of age. At dime size, they are about two months old if they have grown quickly, so you won't have to wait a year. A fish twice as large will only save you about a month.

Raise your grow-out fish in a high tank to protect finnage from fraying. Use a bare tank. A tall 20-gallon (76-L) tank is suitable for a half dozen fish, a 29-gallon (110-L) tank will hold a dozen, and a 55-gallon (208-L) tank is sufficient for two dozen fish. These are starting rates with dime-sized angels; as they grow, you may need to separate them further. I recommend high tanks for long-finned varieties, but in fact all angelfish, even wild-types, have prolonged soft rays in the dorsal, anal, and pelvic fins, and a high tank will keep them intact, whereas a short tank will cause them to wear down to stubs. If you want show fish, use high tanks at all stages.

Breeding Behavior

At about ten months of age, your angelfish will segregate into pairs. Each pair (there may be only one) will occupy one side of the aquarium and drive the other angelfish away. Members of a pair seldom display to one another, instead orienting side-by-side facing outward and threatening the other fish. At this point, the other fish should be removed from the tank (changing the grow-out tank to a breeding tank), or the pair netted and placed in its own dedicated breeding tank. Commercial breeders use the latter method for more efficient use of tank space, but home aquarists who remove the nonbreeders will find that the pair proceeds to spawning more quickly.

Angelfish will pair off in living room community tanks with other fishes, gravel, rooted plants, and other attractive features. It's tempting to remove all other fishes so the pair will breed and raise the young where your entire family can enjoy the spectacle. However, the young require a degree of cleanliness not compatible with an undisturbed, planted tank, which will soon become dirty from heavy feeding. An alternative is to remove the eggs for hatching elsewhere, as in the more efficient procedure described next.

The breeding tank (and grow-out tank) should have a bare bottom, outside filtration, aeration (optional), and a cover. A heater is not necessary in a warm home, but is in a basement or garage. Maintain water quality by frequent (weekly or more often) massive (50 percent or more) water changes. The pH should be held at neutral to slightly basic, and the water should be moderately hard to provide pH buffering. Most municipal water will be hard enough and neutral, but test your water to know if you need to make adjustments. If adjustments are needed, use marine reef buffer salts, or calcium solution, to harden the water and raise the pH to slightly basic. Don't worry about overdosing with hardness chemicals; the more you use, the better control you have of pH, and high levels of hardness will not bother angelfish.

The pair usually selects a nearly vertical surface for egg-laying, a holdover trait from nature where they breed on leaves and stems of tall aquatic plants. The most efficient breeding substratum is a long, narrow strip of plastic or shale or slate rock, but you can also use a length of PVC pipe, a strip of glass, or anything else with a smooth surface. It should be longer than the tank depth, so that it extends the entire water column when leaned against a wall and the bottom. Absent this structure, they'll breed on the side of the tank. Given a live sword plant, they'll almost always select a leaf.

Spawning

Spawning follows days of rigorous scraping and cleaning of the spawning surface by both fish, which use their teeth like steel wool to create the cleanest surface possible. The spawning tubes become engorged and enlarged during cleaning, until the fish are ready to breed.

Breeding is under hormonal control, in turn dependent on temperature, light, a rich diet (see the chapter on feeding), and a cascade of hormones that results, finally, in the female's mature eggs undergoing the process of ripening, during which they take up water and enlarge in preparation for fertilization. No amount of manipulation, feeding, or temperature adjustment will speed up the process; all you can do by environmental manipulation is induce the process. After that, nature takes its inevitable, irrevocable course. If there is any final trigger, it is the withholding of food for one day, which serves the additional purpose of keeping the tank as clean as possible.

Spawning begins with the female seeming to crouch and glide across the spawning substratum, leaving a trail of single-file clear, but prominent (about 1 mm) eggs. She is followed almost immediately by the male making a similar crouching sweep as he deposits milt (sperm) on the eggs, his spawning tube actually rubbing the surface of the eggs as it bounces across them like a fingernail across the teeth of a comb. This contact suggests that the milt is neither especially mobile in water, nor abundant.

Spawning continues, the pair alternating in egg laying and sperm deposition. Spawning may take a couple of hours, and fertilization is not completely assured until the eggs have become turgid and the outer layer (chorion) hardened, about 24 hours later. The eggs are easily damaged by moving them into different quality water within 24 hours of spawning, so wait until the next day.

Caring for the Eggs

You can leave the eggs with the parents, and they will probably raise some of the young. In some cases, the adults may eat the eggs, fail to keep them clean, refuse to feed the fry, or eat the fry. None of these outcomes is likely, as angelfish are among the most devoted parents of any tropical fishes. But your pair might be problem fish. A more likely adverse consequence of leaving the eggs with the parents is that they put all their energies into caring for the young and stop spawning. That's why commercial angelfish breeders remove the eggs for separate hatching and rearing. With their eggs removed, the pair will spawn again usually within 10 days.

If you leave the eggs with the parents for natural hatching, they will take turns fanning and mouthing the eggs to provide aeration and cleaning. They pick away (and eat) dead eggs, so fungal infestations do not occur. There is a risk they will develop a taste for the eggs, in which case you won't get your hatch.

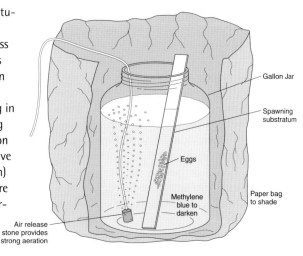

Gallon Jar

Spawning substratum

Eggs

Methylene blue to darken

Paper bag to shade

Air release stone provides strong aeration

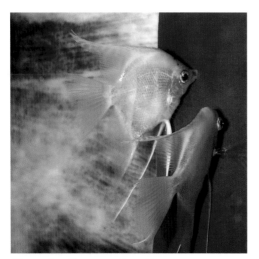

Preparing the spawning site.

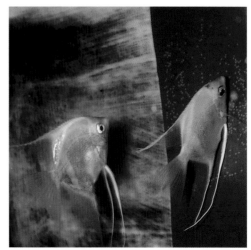

Starting to lay eggs.

Most breeders remove the eggs for mechanical hatching. After 24 hours post-spawning, take the slate, rock, glass, or leaf containing the eggs and put it in a wide mouth gallon jar (available from many fast food and grocery stores) or small bare glass aquarium with clean, new, dechlorinated water (not parent tank water). In a cold house, float or rest the jar inside the temperature-controlled parental aquarium to maintain an even temperature of about 80°F (27°C). If the parental tank is not heated, then the jar need not be either.

Place an air release stone beneath the eggs to send a strong flow of air bubbles over and around the eggs. The bubbles create a strong water flow, providing aeration and washing away debris, and substituting for the fanning and mouthing of the parent fish.

The eggs are light sensitive prior to hatching. You can place the jar inside an opaque paper bag or, alternatively, add methylene blue solution to the water sufficient to tint the water deep, dark

blue. There is no best solution strength, and methylene blue has no antibacterial properties, but neither will it hurt healthy eggs at any concentration. It seems to retard fungal growth (*Saprolegnia*) on infertile eggs, and it is known to have an oxygen carrying capability that may assist the developing embryos.

Darkly stained solution of methylene blue helps protect the eggs during early development.

Laying eggs.

The related discus fish spawns the same way as angelfish, but is more difficult to raise.

From Embryos to Fry

The embryos begin to hatch (wiggling tails penetrating splitting egg shells or chorions) within two days. Some eggs are infertile (opaque white) and become food for fungi, just like mold growing on bread. It's not clear whether the fungal filaments can infect healthy fertilized eggs, but they and the bacteria feeding upon the dead eggs degrade water quality with their microbial wastes, causing stress and sometimes killing the still living fertilized eggs and fry. Opaque and/or eggs coated with fungus should be removed with a turkey baster. Those firmly stuck to the rock amid live developing embryos should be blasted off by shooting water through the baster, and then the debris picked up and discarded.

After the embryos hatch, use a baster or siphon to remove debris and old water from the bottom, and then change half or more of the water by siphoning, or simply tipping the jar. Then slowly (with gravity flow through an airline tube) add new, clean water but no methylene blue to top off the jar.

Baby angelfish quickly shed the egg shells or chorions after hatching, adding to debris. They remain attached to the rock, glass, or leaf and sometimes to one another with adhesive material produced by cement glands on top of the head. The fry, now attached at the head and with tails fiercely beating, create a local flow that assists silt and debris removal and aeration of the water. Equally important, they are

Sexing Angelfish

Angelfish preparing to breed are readily sexed when the tips of the spawning tubes (genital papillae) appear. In the male, the spawning tube, or papilla, at the end of the vas deferens is small, slightly curved, and sharply pointed, like a miniature thorn. In the female, the papilla, or spawning tube, at the end of the oviduct (ovipositor) is broad, not curved, and both blunt and slightly indented at the tip, resembling a miniature volcano. Spawning tubes appear a week or more prior to breeding, but become engorged with blood and enlarged only a day or so before actual spawning.

Angelfish breeders often can pick out mature males and females partly by behavior and partly by the slightly more robust and compact body of the male. Experience is the best teacher; without it, rely on waiting for the tubes to appear.

strengthening muscles by constant exercise. Continue daily partial water changes. Some people don't bother to change water that looks clear and colorless, but metabolic wastes at noxious levels can be colorless. Commercial breeders who practice 80 to 90 percent water

changes every other day obtain rapid growth and excellent production.

At about a week, the fry's cement glands become reduced and the young fish begin disorganized, darting types of experimental swimming that result in more of an exercise for their muscles than in any attempt to get from point A to point B. It will be another day or so until they swim under their own control, their actions related to their perception of food in space.

Artemia nauplii

There is no substitute among tropical fish breeders for newly hatched live brine shrimp, otherwise called nauplii. Brine shrimp (*Artemia*) are small (½ inch [1 cm]) crustaceans that live in desert ponds and lakes with high sodium, calcium, and/or magnesium salt content, where they feed on salt-tolerant blue-green cyanobacteria and algae, and in turn are fed upon by birds. Few other creatures live in salt ponds. In California and elsewhere, seawater is trapped in ponds for drying in the process of making commercial salt, and brine shrimp grow here too.

The eggs of *Artemia* float to the surface of these saline waters and collect in windrows on the lee shores, where they are collected, cleaned, and packaged for the aquaculture market, with about 5 percent diverted to the tropical fish market. These eggs are vacuum canned and may remain viable for years in suspended animation, especially if the cans are stored in a freezer.

When the eggs are immersed in artificial seawater in the light at room temperature or warmer, they hatch in 24 hours, releasing tiny living nauplii. Upon hatching,

Spawning Tubes

Male

Female

the nauplii are rich in nutritious fatty acids, which they quickly use up over the next 24 hours as they double in size. Brine shrimp nauplii should therefore be used upon hatching when they are smallest and most nutritious.

Small packages of brine shrimp eggs are available for sale in pet stores, but I don't buy them. These packages are not airtight, and their eggs are usually damaged by humidity and air, resulting in poor hatches, or none at all. I purchase brine shrimp eggs by the 15-ounce (0.4-kg) vacuum packed can (not plastic package), available from mail-order aquarium and aquaculture suppliers. These eggs, stored in the freezer until use, typically give hatches of 85 to 95 percent and are the choice of breeders.

You can purchase commercial hatching containers, hatch brine shrimp in flat pans, or make hatching jars from inverted soda bottles. However, none of these methods is as simple or efficient as hatching brine shrimp in wide mouth gallon jars with vigorous aeration delivered through a weighted flexible airline tube, or a stiff tube that reaches the bottom. Periodically, the tubing tip must be cleaned of clogging calcium deposits, or simply snipped off for reopening the air passage. With vigorous aeration, there are no dead spots, and you can achieve maximum hatching. Wide mouth jars are also easy to clean.

Follow the directions on the can for making up hatching solutions with uniodized salt, or simply use synthetic seawater. Strong aeration and bright light yield the best hatches. The brine shrimp can be poured through a handkerchief or "brine shrimp net" and the water discarded or recycled. The retained shrimp and egg shells are placed in a half gallon of cold tap water for 30 minutes, during which the shells float to the surface and the nauplii sink to the bottom in a peach-colored mass. Pour off the tap water with the shells, and wipe the remaining shells from the sides of the container with your finger and discard. Then add new tap water to the remaining nauplii, and feed them to the fry with a food baster.

Microworms

Many breeders maintain microworm cultures as a supplemental live food for angelfish (and other tropical fish) fry. Microworms are readily cultured in small covered plastic containers using dried baby food as a food base. Dried Gerber or Pablum flakes are mixed with tap water and a thin paste is spread onto the bottom of a butter or margarine tub to a depth of a half inch. Dried baker's yeast (a live yeast) is sprinkled on top or mixed with the paste. A starter culture of microworms is added to the paste-yeast mixture. The seeded culture is covered with a loose-fitting lid that allows carbon dioxide gas to escape and fresh air to enter. The microworms feed on the yeast, which feed on the baby food. After 24 hours, the yeast and microworms have multiplied profusely.

Within a few days, the microworms are climbing the walls of the container. They are now wiped from the walls with a finger and the finger swirled in a container of tap water. The tap water and microworms are fed to the baby fish. Microworms sink and are ideal for bottom dwelling or weak fry, but strong swimming fry will feed on them from the bottom. Microworms are rich in yeast, a rich source of complex B vitamins. Note that brewer's yeast is a dead yeast preparation and will not support a microworm culture.

Baby angelfish grow quickly with frequent massive water changes and heavy feeding.

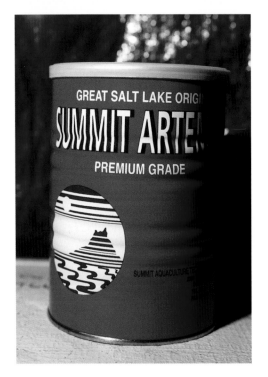

Above: Adult brine shrimp mating and producing eggs.

Left: Vacuum-packed cans of brine shrimp eggs have the best viability and hatch rates.

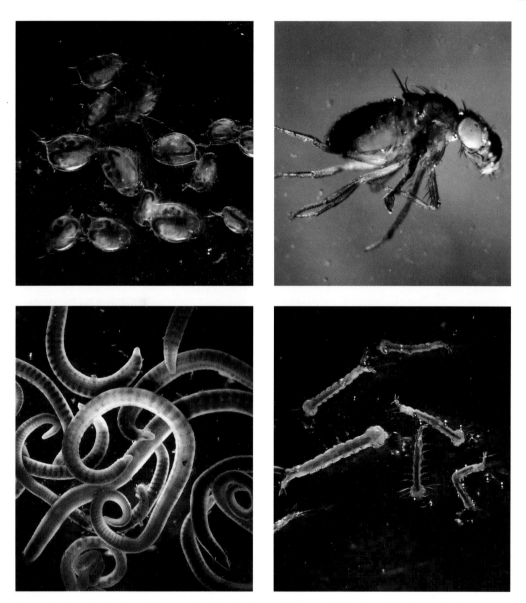

Superior live foods for adult angelfish include daphnia (top left), fruit flies (top right), blackworms (bottom left), and mosquito larvae (bottom right). But frozen foods are adequate and convenient.

Tank Preparation

Prepare a large (20 gallons [76 L] or more) grow-out tank for the hundreds of fry to provide room for growth, heavy feeding, and dilution of wastes between water changes. The tank should be bare, and filtration provided with a sponge filter operated with vigorous aeration. Dechlorinate, allow temperature equilibration, and observe the tank for at least six hours to detect bubbles on the glass. If bubbles appear—indicating supersaturation with air in the tap water—allow the tank to sit and de-gas for another day before use.

Transfer and Feeding of Fry

The grow-out tank and the gallon jar should be at the same temperature. It's a good practice to float the fry jar in the grow-out tank for an hour before the final transfer. If there are few or no air bubbles on the glass, gently transfer the fry into the grow-out tank by immersing and tipping the gallon (4-L) jar. (If you see bubbles forming on the fry, you proceeded too quickly, and the fry may be badly damaged.) By this day or the next, the fry have attained controlled free swimming.

Now begin feeding with newly hatched *Artemia* nauplii. Angelfish fry are large enough to consume baby brine shrimp as a first food, and do not require infusoria. Other nutritious foods are microworms and vinegar eels, but not as staples. Brine shrimp nauplii provides the greatest nutrition and growth, and is the staple of all breeders around the world. Do not be tempted to feed powdered dry foods or liquid fry preparations hawked at pet stores and in magazines. Rely on live baby brine shrimp, combined with continued frequent, massive water changes, and you will easily raise many healthy fry.

Incubating Eggs

These are not rigid rules, for angelfish fry are adaptable and hardy. If you set up the grow-out tank early, or decide to use an established planted tank for grow-out, you can also move the incubating eggs on their slate, glass, or leaf to this tank, with strong aeration over the eggs, and cover the tank to exclude bright light. This permits the fry to hatch out and go to the free swimming state within the grow-out tank. Should the parents spawn on the tank walls itself, you can remove them to a holding or another breeding tank, and weigh down an air release right below and against the egg mass, then let the eggs hatch in that spawning tank (which now becomes the grow-out tank).

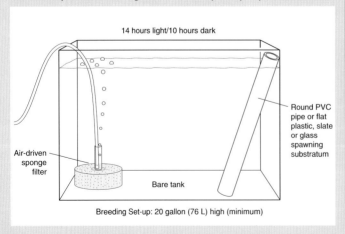

14 hours light/10 hours dark

Round PVC pipe or flat plastic, slate or glass spawning substratum

Air-driven sponge filter

Bare tank

Breeding Set-up: 20 gallon (76 L) high (minimum)

Newborn juveniles can be siphoned into a separate grow-out aquarium: larger juveniles can be transferred by net. The grow-out aquarium should have the same water as that of the parents' aquarium.

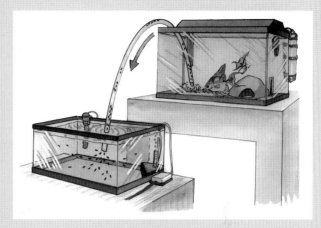

Development of Young Angelfish

After three weeks on live *Artemia* nauplii, you can begin weaning the young on frozen adult brine shrimp. At this time they look like miniature angelfish, and from now on growth is rapid if water changes are contin- ued. The fish may need to be divided among several tanks as they grow. Remove the smallest and the largest to other quarters to avoid any fish being starved. Many breeders discard slow-growing runts, but I do not; they may prove to have other attributes of color intensity, pattern, and finnage that won't show up until later.

Some strains of angelfish are more difficult to raise than others. All-black angels often have high mortality rates. This is probably because they divert much of their amino acid reserve to melanin pigment formation, which creates a deficit in substances needed for neu- rological development.

Optimal Breeding Conditions for Domestic Angelfish

Tank size: 20 to 55 gallons (76 to 209 L)
Photoperiod: 14 hours light, 10 hours dark
Temperature: 80°F (27°C)
pH: 6.8 to 7.4
Hardness: at least 150 ppm or 8.4 degrees German hardness measured with a test kit
Phosphate: undetectable
Ammonia: undetectable
Nitrite: undetectable
Nitrate: undetectable

PTEROPHYLLUM ALTUM PELLEGRIN, 1903

Pterophyllum altum is frequently imported from the wild, but rarely propagated in captivity. This exceptionally tall angelfish with its dramatic red-brown to brown stripes, according to Heiko Bleher, is restricted to western tributaries of the upper Orinoco River on the Colombia–Venezuela border, especially the Rio Inirida at Puerto Inirida, Colombia.

Origin

Pterophyllum altum probably does not occur in eastern tributaries of the Orinoco, or in the Rio Negro, or in any other portions of the Amazon basin, according to several of today's experts. The fact remains, however, that at least one collection reports it from the Rio Negro.

If *P. altum* has indeed crossed from the Orinoco drainage into the Rio Negro, it would have been through a legendary natural connection called the Rio Casiquiare, or the Casiquiare Canal. This high water bridge between the two great rivers was made famous by Alexander von Humboldt, who described it as a fast-moving tributary river of the upper Orinoco that was captured through

land subsidence, causing it to change direction from its original route northward into the Orinoco to its present flow regime, southward into the Rio Negro. This was a dramatic example of stream capture on a massive scale. Later, Alexander Hamilton Rice, the father of photogrammetry, photographed the relationship of the three rivers (Rio Casiquiare, Rio Negro, and Rio Orinoco) from the air. On his last trip in 1924–1925, it is said he ascended the Orinoco River to its headwaters, traversed the natural Casiquiare Canal, and descended the Rio Negro into the Rio Branco, and then continued to the main stem of the Amazon at Manaus. The likelihood of further collections in this area to validate distributions is remote, as the area is now part of the Upper Orinoco/Casiquiare Biosphere Reserve set aside for the stone-age Yanomami native people. The area today is accessible only by foot path or by helicopter, and only by government permit.

Pterophyllum altum, *the tall angelfish.*

Altum Angels

Several populations of angelfish have been called "altum" angels. The status of these fishes, based on conversations with Heiko Bleher, sheds considerable light on the distribution of the true altum angelfish. What of the other "altum" angels from Peru and from the Rio Negro? According to Bleher and others, the Peruvian altum is a high-bodied population of *P. scalare*. Most important, Bleher states that the high-bodied form in the upper Rio Negro that resembles *P. altum* in fact is a variant of *P. scalare*, or something else still unnamed, and it is considerably smaller and less imposing than the true *P. altum*, which occurs only in the Orinoco.

Its habitat, in common with other angelfish, is quiet, densely vegetated, acidic, darkly stained streams and small rivers. Because of its size, it occurs in deeper waters than other angelfish, and Heiko Bleher has seen them in deep water dives where these large fish appeared to be easily 18 to 20 inches (45 to 50 cm) high.

TIP

Unpacking and Transferring Altums

Unpack altums in dim light and float the bags in the quarantine tank for temperature equilibration. After 30 minutes, discard one-fourth of the bag water and replace it with quarantine tank water. Repeat three more times at five minute intervals, discarding shipping and dilution water each time, after which the highly diluted contents of the bag may be poured into the quarantine tank.

Wild quarter-sized immature fish may contain monogenetic trematodes in the gills (gill flukes), or small black spots on the sides caused by melanin depositions around encysted larval digenetic trematodes (*Neascus*). Gill flukes can multiply and cause problems if not eliminated. A five minute seawater dip often eliminates gill flukes in other fishes, but *P. altum* may not tolerate this treatment. Encysted *Neascus* are harmless and need not be treated.

Quarantine

Newly imported *P. altum* should be unpacked in dim light and quarantined in a large volume (20 to 100 gallons [76 to 379 L]) of receiving water in near darkness for the first several days. The receiving water should be soft (DH 1 to 15) and acidic (pH 4.5 to 6.5). Failure to keep them in soft, acidic water may result in susceptibility to bacterial and fungal infections, rapid deterioration, and death. Many newly unpacked fish show no signs of disease, but nonetheless keel over on their sides, do not feed, and die within days. The causes of early mortality are most often shipping stress and failure to place them in the dark in soft, acidic water.

P. altum do best at 82 to 85°F (27 to 29°C), maintained by two high-quality thermostatically controlled heaters. They cannot tolerate chlorine, chloramine, toxic ammonia, or nitrites. Receiving water in the quarantine tank should be dechlorinated/dechloraminated with sodium thiosulfate, ascorbic acid, or another commercial product, and a commercial slime inducer (Amquel, for example) added to assist protection from microbial infections. In acidic water, almost all the ammonia is converted to the nontoxic ammonium ion.

Optimal Breeding Conditions

Tank size: 125 to 300 gallons (473 to 1136 L)
Photoperiod: 14 hours light, 10 hours dark
Temperature: 85°F (30°C)
pH: 4.0 to 6.0
Hardness: less than 50 ppm or 2.8 degrees of
  German hardness using a test kit
Phosphate: undetectable
Ammonia: undetectable
Nitrite: undetectable
Nitrate: undetectable

Shipping water may contain a great deal of waste ammonium ion. If shipping water is added to a receiving tank of neutral pH water, the ammonium ion is converted to toxic ammonia with a rapidly lethal effect. Altums are unlikely to tolerate high levels of nitrites and nitrates. During quarantine, they may develop minor bacterial fin damage that can be safely treated with one of the furan antimicrobials dissolved in water, replenished with water changes daily. Use sponge filtration only. Feed only live adult *Artemia*, *Daphnia*, mosquito larvae, glass worms, white worms, grindle worms, or washed tubificid worms in small quantities twice or more a day, removing uneaten food. *Corydoras* catfish, in the bare quarantine aquarium, will remove excess food.

Grow-out

After two weeks in quarantine the altum angels may be moved into an established, vegetated, 55- to 70-gallon (209- to 265-L) aquarium at 82 to 85°F (27 to 29°C), where the nitrogen fixing bacteria convert nitrites to nitrates and the rich population of plants takes up the nitrates produced. Continue frequent partial water changes to dilute excess nitrates, phosphates, dissolved organic substances, and other waste products.

The grow-out aquarium for quarter-sized wild fish should be not less than 20 gallons (76 L) for six fish, with 55 gallons (209 L) preferable. The tank should have a gravel bottom to support a good population of large rooted plants, such as melon swords or radicans swords, and a population of floating plants such as water sprite to provide some shade. Add a few *Corydoras* catfish to take up uneaten food. The large leaves of the sword plants and surface growths of water sprite provide shade.

The water must be soft and acidic. If topping off evaporated water, use R.O., D.I., or distilled water to avoid inadvertently increasing the hardness. Stain the water with blackwater tonic or peat moss extract to create a yellow-brown tint. Provide strong overhead light to accelerate plant growth and maintain plant health. A trickling filter will provide the best conversion of ammonia to nitrite and nitrite to nitrate, but sponge and outside filtration may be adequate if water changes are frequent and massive. Altums come from quiet water, so do not use current generating powerheads, canister filters, large hanging filters, or strong aeration. Provide a strip of slate, ceramic, or rock leaning against the glass at an angle of 45° for an additional spawning substratum.

Continue feeding live foods only the first week in the grow-out tank, thereafter adding frozen adult brine shrimp, bloodworms, and mysid shrimp (optional) to the live food feedings to wean them off dependence on live food only, and to increase the richness of the diet provided by mysids and bloodworms. Later they may be maintained entirely on frozen foods. Do not feed flake, pellet, stick, granular, or freeze-dried foods that remain partly uneaten and fall to the gravel, where they decay and degrade water quality.

Breeding

Few reliable reports exist of *P. altum* spawning in captivity, and some experts believe it still has not been accomplished. The reports that seem to be reliable were not published, but are reported here from personal communication or Internet sources. All these reports agree that the tank must be large (in excess of 100 gallons [380 L]), and the water strongly acidic, soft, and warm. Multiple fish appear to stimulate

Pterophyllum altum, *the tall angelfish.*

spawning, perhaps by an increase in the concentration of chemical cues.

In an Internet report, Younkger (undated) and Blanco (undated) reported that adult *P. altum* kept in groups paired off, defended a territory, and began scraping a leaf in a manner similar to common angels. At this time they removed the supernumerary fish to another aquarium, leaving the original tank to the breeding pair. Lowering the water level 25 percent for two weeks followed by replacement all at once with slightly cooler distilled or R.O. (reverse osmosis) water, triggered spawning.

Richard Smaciarz (personal communication) reported a spawn of what he believed to be 4 to 5 year old true *P. altum* based on their size (10 to 12 inches [254 to 305 mm] between dorsal and anal fins) and the hooked (indented) snout. His wild fish were purchased at silver dollar body size (one year of age?) from a Minneapolis-St. Paul area wholesaler who was unable to provide the collection locality. Smaciarz's fish were in a 150-gallon (568-L) aquarium, the two pairs separated by an egg crate tank divider. Of the pair that spawned, the female was the larger fish. Water quality conditions were 82°F (28°C), pH 4.75, and German hardness of approximately 1 degree. The fish were conditioned on live earthworms and black worms, and frozen krill, brine shrimp, and bloodworms. They also received spirulina-containing flake food and live *Artemia* nauplii.

At this writing, only a single spawn was discovered, the eggs laid on the glass and top of a 200-watt aquarium heater. The heater was removed for artificial incubation. A few eggs on the plastic dial on top developed into wigglers, were removed, and two are currently being raised with young of a black strain of *P. scalare*. The remainder of the approximately 100 eggs were apparently destroyed by the heating element sometime between the date of spawning and their discovery. The eggs were reported to be about twice as large as *P. scalare* eggs, and the fry described as incredibly active and strong swimmers at an earlier stage than found in *P. scalare*.

Marc Weiss (personal communication) stated that the true *P. altum* has reddish brown bars, attains close to 20 inches (51 cm) in height, and behaves as and is a communal spawner, quite unlike the pair-spawning *P. scalare*. A large number (about 30 adults) held in a 300-gallon (1140-L) tank spawned, several females cleaning the back glass of the aquarium simultaneously, and up to three males contributing to the group spawning. When kept in soft, slightly acid water (pH 6.0), males developed red bars, red spots, and red fins.

The reports by Smaciarz and Weiss do not conflict, but probably represent willing spawners under different conditions. In both cases, multiple fish were in chemical contact, the fish spawned on a vertical surface, and spawning took place in exceptionally large aquariums able to accommodate the height of these tall fish.

Part of the confusion about this fish is caused by unreliable publications. Azuma (1994) reported spawning of *P. altum* from stock collected in the middle Rio Orinoco, the locality forming part of the basis of his presumed identification. His fish spawned in a manner similar to *P. scalare*. Azuma did not

Pterophyllum altum, *the tall angelfish.*

measure fin rays and scale rows. His photographs show a fish with a barely indented snout profile, black rather than brown bars, no distinct intermediate bars, and an exceptionally high body form. Based on the shape of the snout, lack of intermediate bars, black bar color, and no data on meristics, this fish in my opinion, is not *P. altum*, but is most likely a high body *P. scalare* (or undescribed species) similar to the Peruvian "altum" that also occurs in the Rio Orinoco.

References

Azuma, H. "Spawning altum angels." *Tropical Fish Hobbyist* **43**(10)(1994):70–76.

Goldstein, R.J. *Cichlids of the World*. Neptune, NJ: T.F.H. Publications, 1973.

Gratzek, J.B., and J.R. Matthews, eds., *Aquariology, Fish Diseases and Water Chemistry*. Blacksburg, VA: Tetra Press, 1992.

Killino, T.J., and M.S. Bodri. "Safety of Milbemycin as an Oral or Bath Treatment for the Tropical Freshwater Angelfish *Pterophyllum scalare*." *Journal of Zoo and Wildlife Medicine* **28**(1) (1997):94–96.

Mayland, H.J. "The Revalidation of *Pterophyllum leopoldi*." *Tropical Fish Hobbyist* **44**(3) (1995):172–174.

Noga, E. J. *Fish Disease: Diagnosis and Treatment*. St. Louis, MO: Mosby Co. 1995.

Norton, J. "Angelfish Breeding and Genetics." *The Aquarium* **4**(10)(1971):34–41.

Norton, J. "Green Angelfish and Colorful Discus." *The Aquarium* **54**(1)(1971):8–13.

Norton, J. "Angelfish Breeding Tips." *Freshwater and Marine Aquarium* **4**(8)(1981):34–36, 79–80.

Norton, J. "Angelfish Genetics. Part One." *Freshwater and Marine Aquarium* **5**(4)(1982): 15–18, 90–91.

Norton, J. "Angelfish Genetics. Part Two." *Freshwater and Marine Aquarium* **5**(5)(1982): 22–23.

Norton, J. "Angelfish Genetics. Part Three." *Freshwater and Marine Aquarium* **5**(7)(1982): 8–10, 91–92.

Norton, J. "Angelfish Genetics. Part Four." *Freshwater and Marine Aquarium* **5**(8)(1982):15–17.

Norton, J. "Angelfish Genetics. Part Five." *Freshwater and Marine Aquarium* **5**(9)(1982): 8–10.

Norton, J. "Angelfish Genetics. Part Six." *Freshwater and Marine Aquarium* **5**(10)(1982):38–40.

Norton, J. "Angelfish Genetics. Part Seven." *Freshwater and Marine Aquarium* **5**(11)(1982): 40–41.

Norton, J. "Clown Angelfish. *Freshwater and Marine Aquarium* **6**(5)(1983):15–17, 88–91.

Norton, J. "Black Velvet Angelfish." *Freshwater and Marine Aquarium* **7**(7)(1984):10–11.

Norton, J. "Leopard Angelfish." *Freshwater and Marine Aquarium* **8**(2)(1985):10–14.

Norton, J. "Half-black Angelfish." *Freshwater and Marine Aquarium* **8**(8)(1985):18–23.

Norton, J. "Gold Marble Angelfish." *Freshwater and Marine Aquarium* **11**(9)(1988):88–90.

Norton, J. "Half-black Combinations in Angelfish." *Freshwater and Marine Aquarium* **12**(5)(1989):26–28, 134.

Norton, J. "Seven Kinds of Marble Angelfish." *Freshwater and Marine Aquarium* **13**(5)(1990): 127–135.

Norton, J. "Pearly, a New Angelfish Mutation." *Freshwater and Marine Aquarium* **13**(12)(1998): 90–92.

Norton, J. "Fish Genetics, " In *Aquariology, Fish Breeding and Genetics*. Morris Plains, NJ: Tetra Press, 19–58.

Rodger, H.D., M. Kobs, A. Macartney, and G.N. Frerichs. "Systemic Iridovirus Infection in Freshwater Angelfish, *Pterophyllum scalare*." *Journal of Fish Diseases* **20**(1)(1997):69–72.

Staeck, W., and H. Linke. *American Cichlids II. Large Cichlids (updated and revised)*. Blacksburg, VA: Tetra Second Nature, 1995.

Thatcher, V. Amazon Fish Parasites. *Amazoniana* **11**(3,4)(1991):263–571.

Thatcher, V. *Trematodeos Neotropicais*. Manaus, Brazil: Instituto Nacional de Pesquisas da Amazonia, 1993.

+ symbol for the wild-type allele

accession number registration number of a museum specimen

acidic having a pH well below 7.0

albino lacking melanin pigment

alkalinity having the capacity to neutralize acids

alleles genes affecting the same character differently

anal fin unpaired fin on the abdomen of a fish

ascites swelling or bloating with intracellular fluid

bands vertical markings

basic having a pH well above 7.0

B-cell type of antibody-producing white blood cell

blackwater darkly stained soft water

blending incomplete dominance

bloom population explosion

carnivore meat-eater

carrier heterozygous individual with a recessive gene masked by a dominant allele for that trait

caudal fin tail fin

chloride cell specialized gill cell that regulates salt balance

chorion tough outer layer of a fertilized egg

chromosomes paired structures containing DNA from both parents

cichlid member of the Cichlidae

Cichlidae the family of fishes to which angelfishes belong

clinoptilolite type of clay that removes ions from water

conductivity ionic content of water caused by mineral salts

cyanotoxins toxins produced by cyanobacteria (blue-green algae)

cytokinins substances produced by white blood cells to kill bacteria

cytomegaly having abnormal giant cells

deionized (D.I.) water softened through removal of cations by ionic attraction

detritus dead plant fragments

diploid chromosomes that are paired, also denoted as $2n$

DNA deoxyribonucleic acid, the material of genes

dominant gene that masks the effect of its allele

dorsal fin unpaired fin on the back of a fish

double dose homozygous

epistasis interaction of non-allelic genes

epithelium outer cells lining the skin, gills, and intestine

ethologist scientist who studies animal behavior

exophthalmia protruding eyes, as though popping out of the head

exudate leakage from a wound, often pus and microbes

gamete sperm cell or egg cell

gene unit of inheritance, a sequence of DNA

geneticist scientist who studies genetics

genetics science of inheritance

genome all the genes of a species

genotype genes an individual has for a specific trait

genus first word of a two-part scientific name

germinal cell diploid precursor of haploid egg or sperm cell

Gondwana ancient land mass that fractured into modern continents

gut intestinal tract

habitat characteristic environment of a species

haploid having just one chromosome of each pair, also denoted n

Wild angelfish resembling Pterophyllum altum, *but perhaps a variant of* Pterophyllum scalare. *Scales were not counted.*

hard water having a high concentration of dissolved calcium

herbivore plant-eater

heterozygote being heterozygous

heterozygous having two different alleles of a gene

holotype original specimen in a museum given a species name, and representative of a natural population believed to be distinct from all other known fishes

homozygote being homozygous

homozygous having a pair of identical alleles

HUFA highly unsaturated fatty acid

humic acid substance leached from dead vegetation

hyperplasia abnormal cell multiplication

hypertrophy abnormal cell enlargement

ichthyologist scientist who studies fishes

incomplete dominant gene that blends its effects with those of an allele

iridocyte cell containing iridophores

iridophores structures with iridescent guanine crystals

isozymes similar enzymes having similar activities

junior synonym invalid name because the species was described earlier

lateral line pored flank scales containing sensory structures

lesion damaged tissue, a wound or sore

lipids fats (solid) and oils (liquid)

loci more than one locus

locus specific position of allele on its chromosome

magma molten rock from the interior of the planet

maturation attaining sexual maturity, the ability to reproduce

medicament veterinary drug

meiosis division of germinal cells to form haploid sperm or egg cells

meristics counts of fin rays and scales

microbes bacteria (and fungi)

milt fish sperm

mitochondria structures in the cytoplasm where oxygen is used, toxins are neutralized, and special genes inherited only from the mother are located

mitosis normal division of diploid (body) cells

morphometrics body proportions

mouthbreeding mouthbrooding

mouthbrooding incubating fertilized eggs in the mouth cavity

nauplii larvae of brine shrimp and some other crustaceans

nucleic acids components of DNA

osteology study of skeletal systems

paratype additional specimen to accompany holotype

pathogenicity ability to cause disease

pathology study of disease

PCR polymerase chain reaction

pectoral fins paired fins located near the throat of a fish

pelvic fins paired fins located near the anus of a fish

pH numerical value of acidity or basicity

phagocyte engulfing and digesting white blood cell

phenotype appearance of an individual

phylogenetic tree diagrammatic representation of how related modern animals descended from their ancestors

phylogeny *see* phylogenetic tree

plate tectonics movement of continents over the surface of the planet

polymerase chain reaction laboratory technique for making vast amounts of a gene in multiplying bacteria

ray flexible or soft segmented fin support

recessive gene that is masked by the effect of an allele

rifting separation of tectonic plates

R.O. water softed by reverse osmosis through a membrane that blocks cations

sedimentary derived from ancient silts

sediments settled particles, usually silts

septicemia bacterial blood poisoning

soft water having virtually no dissolved calcium or other cations

species name of the holotype

specific epithet second word of a two-part scientific name

spine hard, unsegmented fin support

stream capture headwater stream of one river erodes or subsides into a separate drainage, causing the water of one of them to reverse flow to follow gravity

substrate substance affected by a chemical reaction

substratum bottom or base of a water body

synonym junior synonym

tannin tannic acid, leached from vegetation

taxonomy system of naming plants or animals

T-cell type of antibody-producing white blood cell

tectonic plate discrete segment of earth's crust derived from hardening magma pouring from a rift, the plate drifts over the surface of the planet, and may carry either sea floor or a continent

tetanus muscle cramping

total evidence analysis statistical analysis using many branches of science to interpret phylogentic relationships

toxic poisonous

trade name common name created by dealers and wholesalers

type specimen holotype or equivalent

undescribed species fish not yet described in a publication and having no valid scientific name

ventral fins pelvic fins

virulence degree of pathogenicity

white blood cells T-cells, B-cells, and phagocytes

white water turbid or silt-laden water

zygote fertilized egg

Acknowledgments
I'm grateful to many unselfish individuals for leads and literature, facts and photographs, reviews and research, and doing their darndest to keep me pointed at pertinent information. My special thanks to Heiko Bleher, John Gratzek, Dean Hougen, Sven Kullander, Joanne Norton, Wayne Leibel, Lee Finley, Frank Schäfer, Ed Noga, Mike Vaughan, Shannon Coulter, Mary Bailey, and Marc Weiss for relentless corrections and advice. I'm also grateful for the interviews granted by Miami importers Adolf Schwartz, Alberto Salazar, Jose Mantilla Meyer, Michael Rambarran, Julio Galiano, Adolfo Arbulu, and Naz Rahaman.

Cover Credits
All covers by Joanne Norton.

Photo Credits
Robert J. Goldstein: pages 9, 12, 16 (top r), 17 (top), 21 (top), 60, 64 (top l, top r), 65 (top l, top r), 68, 69 (top l, top r, bottom l, bottom r), 72, 76 (bottom), 77 (top l, top r), 80 (top, bottom l, bottom r), 81 (top l, top r, bottom l, bottom r), 88, 92. Aaron Norman: pages 16 (bottom), 20 (bottom l), 21 (bottom l, bottom r), 28 (bottom), 29 (bottom r), 84. Joanne Norton: pages 2, 3, 4, 5, 13, 16 (top l), 17 (bottom), 20 (top l, top r, bottom r), 24, 25, 28 (top l, top r), 29 (top, bottom l), 32, 33, 36, 40, 41, 44 (top l, top r, bottom l, bottom r), 45 (top l, top r, bottom l, bottom r), 48, 49, 52 (top l, middle l, bottom l, top r, bottom r), 53 (top, middle l, middle r, bottom l), 56, 57, 61, 73, 76 (top l, top r), 85, 89.

Author's Note
For this book I interviewed fish scientists, collectors, importers, adventurers, breeders, and experts in the study of tropical fishes. I have relied heavily on my own experience with *Pterophyllum scalare* (I was keeping them before George W. Bush was born.) And I have expanded this knowledge by relying on geneticists, disease experts, the community of Miami importers, and European scientists and explorers. What I have written is, I hope, the most reliable handbook yet for understanding *Pterophyllum scalare*, and a reasoned assessment of our understanding of the other species and populations of wild angelfishes.

All inquiries should be addressed to:
Barron's Educational Series, Inc.
250 Wireless Boulevard
Hauppauge, New York 11788
http://www.barronseduc.com

International Standard Book No. 0-7641-1661-4

Library of Congress Catalog Card No. 2001025167

Library of Congress Cataloging-in-Publication Data

Goldstein, Robert J. (Robert Jay), 1937–
Angelfish : a complete pet owner's manual : everything about purchase, care, nutrition, behavior, and aquarium maintenance / Robert J. Goldstein.
     p.   cm.
     ISBN 0-7641-1661-4 (alk. paper)
     1. Scalare.   I. Title.
SF458.S34. G65   2001
636.3'772—dc21   2001025167

Printed in Hong Kong

9 8 7 6 5 4 3 2 1